The Banker's Friend

– DANIEL REALE–

An environmentally friendly book printed and bound in England by
www.printondemand-worldwide.com

Mixed Sources
Product group from well-managed forests, and other controlled sources
www.fsc.org Cert no. TT-COC-002641
© 1996 Forest Stewardship Council
FSC

PEFC Certified
This product is from sustainably managed forests and controlled sources
PEFC
PEFC/16-33-415
www.pefc.org

This book is made entirely of chain-of-custody materials

FastPrint Publishing
www.fast-print.net/store.php

The Banker's Friend

ISBN 978-184426-990-7

First published 2011 by
FASTPRINT PUBLISHING
Peterborough, England.

THE BANKER'S FRIEND

A basic and not so basic financial tool

Daniel Reale

CONTENTS

PREFACE

The aftermath of 2007/2010 …

"Bankers' bashing"

Ok, over the past few years, some senior bankers have been greedy and irresponsible in their approach to risk-taking;
Not only with their own money but quite regularly with their clients' money …
So we need reforms and regulations but not excessive ones …
Fiduciary duty and claw backs would be a good start …

However, they cannot be blamed for everything …
People from every walk of life must accept some responsibility; as greed is the deadly sin…

Anyway, like them or loathe them, we need them…

INTRODUCTION

To my son Marc

This book has been compiled with you, the young professional, in mind …

It is *not a recipe* on how to invest but a *benchmark* and a *working tool* for the banking professional.
It is all about the ins and outs of the trade.
Here, its intricate mechanisms are explained …

Very often we can hear: "What does "this" mean?"
Here you have the answer!
However, it's much more than a glossary …
Not only technical words are explained in detail but they are accompanied with ample examples.

If you want to be one step ahead of your colleagues, this *working tool* is a must; you can't do without it …

To start with…

We cannot talk about finance without mentioning capitalism …

WHAT IS CAPITALISM?

Capitalism is an economic system in which the means of production are *privately owned* (not by governments or communities) and operated for *profit.*

A capitalist society is *ruled by money* and *those who possess* it.

Capitalism applies the natural rules of survival of the fittest …

To put it bluntly, in the twenty first century, capitalists are at war …competitors are the enemies that have to be destroyed, annihilated by any means and at any costs (legally and sometimes illegally…).
Lots of 21st century capitalists are financial sharks…

However it must be said that the bailing-out of some of the biggest financial institutions by the state and tax payers (2008/2009) has been "a slap in the face" of capitalism…

Anyway, as a capitalist society…

WE ALL NEED MONEY AND CREDIT…

Let it be you and me (as individuals) or a going concern (like a corner shop) or a big business (like a listed company) or a government … *we all need money ... and credit ...*

If we do not have money or enough of it, we *borrow* some …
We *borrow* money to *make money* or to get *more of it* …
Sometimes it is for a good reason (for example re-investing in an existing business or to make it more competitive) but more often, it is out of *sheer greed …*
The more money we have, the more we want …

How to get it is one of our main worries and occupations …
Either we inherit it, win it, steal it, earn it through hard work, borrow it or get it through "witty" *investments …*

An individual or a business' owner may ask their retail/commercial bank for help…
A big company (especially the listed one) may turn to its shareholders or ask an *investment bank* to help it raise money on the financial markets…
A government may borrow money through the issuance of gilts…
A bank may borrow money from another bank to lend it and make a profit…

Money - greed - borrowing - lending - credit – investing, speculating and *profit and loss* are the *driving words* of the financial world... more so after "*City Big Bang*"

CITY BIG BANG

In 1986 (Lady Thatcher's government) the sudden *deregulation* of financial markets came to be known as Big Bang.

The package of reforms did a few things:

For one, *it broke down the barrier* that until then kept brokers, who traded shares on behalf of their clients and the market makers, separate.
It also eliminated fixed commissions and it allowed *foreign ownership of UK brokers* for the first time.

Out went long business lunches and in came American banks, electronic trading and the cut-throat competitive ethos that has put London at the heart of the world of finance.

The main beneficiaries:
The City, the companies, the banks and the institutional investors like pension funds, mutual funds, hedge funds, private equity companies, etc... together with the retail and private investors.

DIFFERENT TYPES OF BUSINESS

Now, there are different types of businesses and companies and different types of banks with different roles and functions. Moreover, many banks have multiple divisions covering some or all of these roles and functions.

We will be looking at some of the *main financial players* but first let us differentiate a sole trader from a company…

What is a Sole trader?

Being a sole trader is a great way to start a business.
It's quick, inexpensive.
However, you're *personally responsible* for any losses the business makes.
The bigger your business gets, the greater the benefits of becoming *a limited company.*
Then the company, not you as an individual, is liable for business debts.
If you're becoming liable for an increasing number or total of expenses, you should consider *limited-company status.*
This can protect you from bankruptcy if you can't afford to pay your debts.
Your liability is normally *limited* to the amount you invest in the company.
Limited-company status can also give potential customers the impression that your business is more established and larger than it is.
As *a sole trader*, you might employ 50 people, but still be seen as *a one-man band.*

THE MAIN FINANCIAL PLAYERS

The companies

A company is a legal entity formed to conduct business or other activities in the name of the association.

There are four main types of company:

- *Private company limited by shares*

This type of company has a *share capital* and the liability of each member to creditors *is limited* to the amount originally invested.

A company limited by shares is the conventional and most well known type of limited company.
The company issues shares and the profits can be distributed to shareholders as a dividend.
A private company cannot offer its shares for sale to the general public.

- *Private company limited by guarantee*

In this type of company, members do not make any contribution to the capital during its lifetime as they do not purchase shares.
The members' liability is limited to the *amount* that they each *agree* to contribute to the company's assets if it is wound up.

A company limited by guarantee is the conventional type of company for a "not for profit" organization such as an association or a club.
This type of company does not issue shares and profits are not distributed to the members.

Note: *One-person private company* (limited by shares or guarantee) *does* exist and is legal.
The same person may be sole director and shareholder.

- *Private unlimited company*

This type of company may or may not have a share capital and there is no limit to the members' liability. Because there is no limitation on members' liability, the company has to disclose less information than other types of company.

- *Public limited company*

This type of company has a *share capital* and the liability of each shareholder to creditors *is limited* to the amount originally invested (like a Private company limited by shares).
It means that those who run and finance them *cannot lose more than their investment.*

The main reason for forming a *public* company is *to raise capital for expansion;* as it has access *to capital markets.*

A public limited company may offer its shares for sale to the general public.
It may also be *quoted/listed on a stock exchange* (through an *Initial Public Offering)* – giving the company more borrowing power and *some prestige...*

Public companies require a minimum capital investment (£50,000 in 2010).

Notes

- Unlike a public company, a private firm doesn't have to answer to shareholders.

- The norm is for new companies, which are typically small, to be privately owned.
After a number of years, if a company has grown significantly and is profitable, or has promising prospects, there is often an initial public offering which converts the private company into a public company or an acquisition of a company by public company.

- Usually, the securities of a public company are owned by many investors while the shares of a private company are owned by relatively few shareholders.
However, a company with many shareholders is not necessarily a public company.

The banks

Like them or loathe them, we need them …

Banks can be divided into three main bodies:

- *Central banks*
- *Retail/commercial banks*
- *Investment banks*

A central bank

It is "normally" government-owned and charged with "quasi-regulatory responsibilities", such as issuing the currency, supervising retail/commercial banks and controlling the cash interest rate.

A central bank generally provides liquidity to the banking system and act as the *lender of last resort in event of a crisis.*

Central bank rate

The bank rate is set by a special Bank of England committee, known as the Monetary Policy Committee (MPC) that meets at the beginning of each month.

The central bank rate acts as a *"bench-mark"* for the money market and financial institutions like banks and for building societies for their own savers and borrowers.

Changes to interest rate

When the MPC decides to change the official interest rate, it is attempting *to influence* the overall level of activity in the economy.

It seeks to keep a healthy balance between supply and demand across the UK economy.

A *falling central bank rate* usually *weakens* a country's currency and may leave its currency *less attractive* to foreign investors.
A *reduction* in interest rates makes *saving less attractive* and *borrowing more so* and thereby helps to stimulate spending and investment.
It makes it easier for businesses to export goods and services.

Higher rates, of course, have the opposite effect.

However, during the financial crisis and the credit crunch (2007/2009), successive *cuts* to the *bank basic rate* (down to 0.5%) failed to get the economy moving again…
So the Bank of England together with the Treasury had to resort to *capital injection* and *quantitative easing* to bail-out banks and kick-start the economy…
They bought shares and bonds from banks in difficulty.

Note
Every retail/commercial bank *holds an account* with their central bank; which is very handy for bailing out the ones in difficulty - capital injection and quantitative easing (the "virtual"/"electronic" printing of money).

Retail/commercial banks.

They execute transactions *directly with consumers*, rather than corporations or other banks.

Services offered include: savings accounts, current accounts, mortgages, personal loans (secured or unsecured), business loans, advice on personal investment like investment funds, shares and bonds, credit card facilities and so on.

Now, have you ever asked yourself how banks can afford so much money and where they get it from?

- The high street banks "borrow" money from *saving* and *current accounts* to trade…
  They pay let's say 2.5% interest on a saving account and lend this money at say 5% …
- They borrow money through the issuance of *bonds;* selling these bonds with a 3% interest and use this money to lend at say 8%...
- They borrow from other banks at very competitive rates and again make huge *profit from the spread* (difference)…
- They impose heavy *fees* on credit cards, overdraft, etc…
- They charge hefty rates for mortgages, other personal loans and business loans**…**
- They trade for themselves - proprietary trading - (sometimes with your money).

It is as simple as this!...

Now let's see how the investment banks get it…

Investment banks (corporate finance).
Investment banks work for and profit from companies and governments (local and central) by helping them *raise money* in capital markets (*underwriting* the issuance of both equity and debt) and by providing advice on transactions such *as mergers and acquisitions* and *IPOs* (Initial Public Offerings).

Note: For them, it is a very lucrative job …as they are paid huge fees for doing deals *rather than* for *successful* ones …

They also assist their clients in the *trading of derivatives, fixed incomes (like bonds), foreign exchange, commodity and equity securities.*

Furthermore they provide ancillary services such as *risk management advice* and *corporate lending.*

Note: Investment banks are not only *broker dealers* but are also *market makers* (quoting both a buy and a sell price in a financial instrument or commodity) - making good profit from the *spread...*

Moreover, investment banks trade and invest for themselves (*proprietary trading*).
They trade heavily in derivatives, foreign exchange, commodity and equity securities … together with running hedge funds and investing in private equity.
For example, they buy and sell between them billions of pounds of gold and foreign currencies every day…

Note: - Volker's rule - Aug 2010 – "Congress put a curb on US investment banks" - Proprietary trading is banned…
Will Europe follow suit?

An investment bank structure/organization

An investment bank is split into the so-called *front office, middle office and back office.*

Front office

Corporate finance:

Companies use the investment banking division to help them *raise capital* through the *issuing* and *underwriting* of *shares and bonds.*

Another key area is advising companies on *mergers and acquisitions and IPOs (Initial Public Offerings).*

Capital markets:

On behalf of the bank and its clients, the primary function of a large investment bank is buying and selling products.

This is where the banks trade bonds, shares/equities, derivatives, commodities, foreign exchange and other securities.

In market making, *traders* will buy and sell financial products with the goal of making a profit.

Note: a *market maker* is an individual, that quotes both a buy and a sell price for a financial product.

Research:

Analysts review companies and write reports about their prospects and often advise with "buy" or "sell" ratings.

However, there is a *potential conflict of interest* between the investment bank and its analysis in that published analysis can affect the profits of the bank.

So the relationship between investment banking and research has become highly regulated and a *Chinese wall* is now a must.

Middle office

Risk management - Financial control (with cash management) - Compliance with regulations.

Back office

Operations involve data-checking trades that have been conducted, ensuring that they are not erroneous and the required transfers are duly transacted.

Clearing and settlement are also important "back-office" post-trade activities.

IT department

Notes - *There are three types of trading and traders:*
Proprietary, flow (market makers) and sales:

Proprietary traders trade on behalf of the *bank itself* (with the bank's money and controversially sometimes with their clients').
Their aim is to buy low and sell high.
They do this by analysing economic data, technical analysis, experience and identifying undervalued and overvalued prices.

Flow traders buy and sell products on the financial markets for the *bank's clients* (institutional investors and central/local government).
Products include securities and other assets such as futures, options and commodities.
They make prices and execute trades, seeking to maximise assets or minimise financial risk.

Sales traders deal directly with clients, providing market information, execution and promoting new financial ideas to clients.
They are intermediaries between the client and the market maker.

To be a trader is a 24/7 job ...
First and foremost, the trader must be aware of what is going on all over the world; taking into consideration political unrests, riots, civil wars, elections, currency fluctuations, weather (flood, drought and monsoon) for commodities like cocoa, coffee and cotton, etc ...

Examples: Oil and Suez Canal, cotton during political unrest in Egypt and gold during the Indian wedding season when the precious metal is in high demand (dowry); as any of these events will affect the supply, demand and price of a particular product...

Other banks

Islamic banks
An Islamic bank adheres to the concepts of Islamic law.
Sharia Law prohibits the payment or acceptance of interest fees for loans of money.
European Central Bank
It is one of the world's most important central banks
Its main objective is to maintain price stability within the Eurozone (to keep inflation low).
European Investment Bank
It provides funding for projects such as roads and power-plant construction in Europe as well as for development projects in poorer countries.
World Bank
It provides loans to developing countries with the money received from the IMF (International Monetary Fund).

The hedge funds

They are firms specializing in *higher-risk, higher-reward* investments for *wealthy clients*.
Hedge funds are often linked to takeovers or other big trades in the financial markets.

They have become big players.
It has been claimed that these *privately owned investment companies* are responsible for half the daily turnover of shares on the London stock market.

Some hedge fund managers will use *derivatives* almost exclusively, such as *Contracts for Difference* (see the words in the "jargon" section), rather than buying the underlying asset directly.

As the name implies, *hedge* funds often seek to *offset* potential losses in the principal markets they invest in by *hedging their investments* using a variety of methods, most notably *short selling.*

Comparisons to private equity funds
The line between Hedge Funds and Private Equity is growing greyer each year and are similar in many respects:

- *Both* are *lightly regulated...*

- Most *hedge funds* invest in relatively *liquid assets* and investors may enter or leave the fund (giving some months notice).

- *Private equity funds* invest primarily in very *illiquid assets* such as early-stage companies.

- *Hedge funds* often invest in private equity companies' acquisition funds.

- Many hedge funds are owned by private equity groups and many private equity firms are making long-term investments in the ownership of hedge funds.

Notes

Redemption is when an investor gets a chance to "*exit*" the fund (*asking* for their cash *money back)*.

Some "reckless" government councils place up to 90% of their pension pots on the stock market and invest thousands in hedge funds...
Many "gamble" millions of pounds of pensioners' money

The private equities – The "buyout" barons …

Private equity firms are essentially *investment companies*. The name "private equity" refers to how they raise the funds they use.
Instead of going to the stock market and selling shares, private equity companies raise funds *from private sources*, usually pension funds and wealthy individuals.

They then use this cash, along with borrowed money (leverage), to buy companies that they have identified as underperforming.
Their aim is to turn the business around and sell it on at a profit at a future date.

Supporters of private equity companies praise their ability to create jobs quickly and contribute to the economy.

Yet others would disagree, most notably employees at companies which have been bought by private equity groups only to see hundreds of job cuts being made …

However, the private equity firms say they simply have to cut jobs to make the companies they buy profitable and then if necessary re-employ people...

Controversial taxation
One of the big objections to private equity is the tax breaks given to the industry; the most controversial being the tax on the "*carry*".
As any other tax payer, private equity executives pay taxes on their basic pay and bonuses, but a large part of their income comes from carried interest - *the carry* - which is the 20% slice of profits they can claim once they have paid back their investors.

This money is classed as a *capital gain* and, thanks to something called *taper relief (entrepreneurs relief),* it is only subject to a tax level of 10%.

Note
Redemption is when an investor gets a chance to "*exit*" the fund (*asking* for their cash *money back).*

Before moving to another paragraph, let us not forget other "*big players*" like pension funds, insurance companies and local governments.

Let's now look at the financial markets and at some financial instruments:

A FINANCIAL MARKET

It is a mechanism that allows people to buy and sell (trade) financial securities (such as stocks and bonds), commodities (such as gold, oil or cotton), etc...

However, the term "market" is used for what are more strictly exchanges - e.g., *a stock exchange, commodity exchange or foreign exchange.*

But other financial actions like mergers and acquisitions and some derivatives are executed *outside an exchange*.
The same goes for any two companies or people that agree to sell and buy stock, do their trade *without using an exchange*.
Trading of currencies and bonds is largely on a bilateral basis, although some bonds trade on a *stock exchange*…

THE STOCK EXCHANGES/BOURSES

A stock exchange or *bourse* (in Europe) is a corporation which provides "trading facilities" for stock brokers and traders to trade stocks and other securities.

The securities traded on a stock exchange may include: shares, commodities, unit trusts, exchanged traded funds, etc …

Notes

The main reason for listing a public company on to a stock exchange is *to raise capital*, get a positive exposure to the financial world and maybe some prestige…

- There is *no compulsion* to issue stock via the stock exchange itself nor must stock be subsequently traded on the exchange. Trading can be done off exchange or OTC (over-the-counter). OTC is the *usual way* that bonds, derivatives and currencies are traded.

Major stock exchanges

Every industrialized country has at least one stock exchange; many have two, three ...
However, at the beginning of 2011, there has been a frenzy of stock market mergers:
- LSE (which had taken over Turquoise in 2010) has joined forces with TMX (Toronto Metal Exchange).
- Deutsche Börse and NYSE Euronext - the two dominant platforms for the European futures market - could merge in a near future but are facing competition hurdles (and a bid by Nasdaq for NYSE Euronext)...
- A merger between BATS Global Markets and Chi-X Europe is also imminent ...

Other major stock exchanges:
- Bombay stock exchange
- NASDAQ
- NYSE/EURONEXT: Belgium, France (Paris bourse), Netherlands, Luxembourg, Portugal and LIFFE (London International Financial Futures and Options Exchange).
- Hong Kong exchange
- Tokyo stock exchange

The Small Cap markets

- The *AIM market* (Alternative Investment Market) is part of the London Stock Exchange.

Its more flexible regulatory regime allows smaller firms to "come to the market" to raise the needed capital without having

to go through the listing and disclosure requirements that firms listing on the main market have to undertake.
AIM is officially classed as an exchange *regulated* market.

- *PLUS Market* is a relatively new stock exchange based in London for small and mid caps.
Over 8,000 (2010) companies were traded on PLUS, while 200 were quoted.
PLUS has *recognised* investment exchange status; which gives it the same rights and privileges as the London Stock Exchange.

Note
Do not confuse/mix up stock *exchanges* (they provide "trading" facilities like electronic trading platforms for stock brokers and traders to trade stocks and other securities) and *indexes/indices.*

Here are some of the major stock market indexes:

- FTSE is a joint venture between the Financial Times and the London Stock Exchange.
  (FTSE 100 and FTSE 250 … mean the first 100 – 250 companies by market capitalisation)
- Dow Jones (only 30 stocks listed)
- Nikkei – S&P 500
- FTS Eurofirst 300 is a joint product of FTSE Group, the leading global index provider and Euronext, an integrated cross border European exchange for equities, bonds, derivatives and commodities.

FOREX

The Foreign Exchange is an *OTC market* (over the counter, directly between 2 parties) where brokers/dealers negotiate directly with one another; *there is no central exchange or clearing house* (see clearing house).

The FX market is where currency trading takes place.
It is the largest and most liquid financial markets in the world and includes trading between large banks, central banks, currency speculators, corporations, governments and other institutions.
Most foreign exchange trading firms are *market makers*.
In foreign exchange trading, the market maker sells to and buys from its clients and is compensated by means of price differentials.

The primary purpose of the foreign exchange market is to assist international trade and investment …

Foreign exchange market break-down:
- *Spot trading* is buying one currency with a different currency for immediate delivery, rather than for future delivery.
- *Forwards*
- Foreign exchange *Swaps*

All trades in forex are quoted in *pairs* and the *first* currency is called the *base currency*.

Currency pairs move in pips (Price Interest Point)

In essence, that is really it!

OVER THE COUNTER (OTC)

A security traded in some context other than one on a formal exchange such as the LSE, AMEX, etc.
The phrase "over-the-counter" can be used to refer to stocks that trade via a dealer network as opposed to on a centralised exchange.
It also refers to debt securities and other financial instruments such as derivatives (Future contracts - Options – Warrants - CFDs- Spread betting – Bonds etc …), which are traded through a dealer network.
They do not go through a clearing house... See clearing house.

Also known as "unlisted stock", these securities are traded by broker-dealers who negotiate directly with one another over computer networks and by phone.

Be very wary of some OTC stocks, however; the OTC BB stocks are either penny stocks or are offered by companies with bad credit records.

Instruments such as bonds do not trade on a formal exchange and are, therefore, also considered OTC securities.

Most debt instruments (e.g. bonds) are traded by investment banks making markets for specific issues.
If an investor wants to buy or sell a bond, he or she must call the bank that makes the market in that bond and asks for quotes.

THE MAIN FINANCIAL INSTRUMENTS

Financial instruments

They are *tools* to facilitate trading …

They are items like loans, bonds, shares, derivatives like options, etc…

There are two basic types:

> *Cash instruments* are financial instruments whose value is determined *directly* by markets (securities, loans, deposits).
>
> *Derivative instruments* are financial instruments which *derive* their value *from* the value of one or more underlying assets.
>
> They can be divided into *exchange-traded* derivatives and *over-the-counter derivatives*.

Note: *Foreign exchange instruments* and *transactions* are neither debt nor equity based and belong in their own category.

The bonds

When a company needs to raise money, instead of selling shares or asking for a loan, it can issue *bonds*.

When a government needs to raise money it only has two options: Either through direct/indirect taxes or via the issuance of bonds.

A bond is a certificate of *debt* (IOU) issued by a government (gilt) or a corporation (corporate bond) that *guarantees payment of the original investment plus interest by a specified future date.*

Bonds are traded on the open market.

Grouped under the general category called *fixed-income securities*, the term bond (*corporate bond* and government bond or *gilt*) is commonly used to refer to any securities that are founded on *debt.*

When you purchase a bond, you are lending out your money to a company or government.
In return, they agree to give you interest on your money and eventually pay you back the amount you lent out.

Note: Bonds perform differently from shares because they have a fixed life and usually pay a set income or *'coupon'.*

There are many different types of bonds:

- *Fixed rate bonds* have a coupon that remains constant throughout the life of the bond.

- *Zero-coupon bonds* pay no regular interest.

- *Inflation linked bonds*, in which the principal amount and the interest payments are indexed to inflation.

- *Asset-backed securities* are bonds whose interest and principal payments are backed by underlying cash flows from other assets.
Examples of asset-backed securities are mortgage-backed securities (MBS's), collateralized mortgage obligations (CMOs) and collateralized debt obligations (CDOs) like the now infamous sub-prime bonds.

- *Subordinated bonds* are those that have a lower priority than other bonds of the issuer in case of liquidation.

- *Perpetual bonds* are also often called perpetuities or 'Perps'. They have no maturity date.

- *Bearer bond* is an official certificate issued without a named holder. In other words, the person who has the paper certificate can claim the value of the bond.

- A *convertible bond* lets a bondholder exchange a bond to a number of shares of the issuer's common stock

- *Contingent convertible bonds (coco)*
These bonds convert into equity in times of stress, for example if a bank's capital ratio falls below regulatory requirements (Basel III). However, issuers have to pay a premium to take on the risk that their bonds might turn into non-interest-paying equities.
They do not dilute shares upfront and act as *capital buffers.*

- An *exchangeable bond* allows for exchange to shares of a corporation other than the issuer.

- *Retail bond* is relatively new and it is one which is available to private individuals (on line) rather than confined to major City investors.
It allows private investors to buy and sell corporate bonds or gilts as easily as they can trade shares, on the LSE, for as little as £100.
However, bear in mind the dealing charges to your broker:
If you are buying a £100 bond with a 5% yield (interest) and the cost of the transaction is £10 then you will immediately be sacrificing two years of income

- *Eurobonds* (not to be confused with the new E-bonds)
Eurobonds are international bonds that are denominated in a currency not native to the country where they are issued.
Eurobonds may be traded throughout the world.

Eurobonds are named after the currency they are denominated in (Eurodollar bonds for example).

- *E-bonds* (*region-wide* Eurozone bonds) are new bonds issued by the European Commission and are backed by Europe's most stable economies.

- *Sovereign bonds*
A debt security issued by a *national government* within a given country and denominated in a *foreign currency.*

- *Premium bonds* are like a safe government-backed lottery. Each bond is entered into a monthly prize draw, the size of which is based on current interest rates.
The government promises to buy back the bond, on request, for its original price.
However, there is no interest paid on Premium bonds.
The advantage being that you can keep your Premium bonds forever …

Notes
- An *investment-grade bond* is a low-risk corporate bond (at least a BBB rating) because the bond issuer has a good credit rating.
The issuer is usually a government which is highly unlikely to default.

- A *junk bond* is a high-risk bond because the issuer has a poor credit rating (BB or lower) and therefore is more likely to default.

Bond *price*: (Not to be confused with bond *yield*) It is the amount an investor *pays to buy* a bond.

Bond *yield*: It is the *percentage return* an investor would earn if a bond was purchased and held to maturity.

Usually, the longer the term of a bond, the higher the interest rate that's paid to the holder, compensating for the inflation risk of having money tied up for a long time.

Yield example:
If you bought a bond at a *discounted price* (below the face value), your yield would be *higher* than the rate:
You buy a bond on Jan 1 with a face value of £1,000 and a stated rate of 5% (annual interest payment) at the discounted price of £950.
On Dec 31 *(after 12 months)*, you receive £50 in interest (1,000 x 5%) which gives you a 5.26% *yield* (50/950 per cent).

Or, if you bought a bond for face value *close to the coupon date,* your yield would be *higher* than the rate as well…
On July 1, you pay the face value of £1,000 for a bond with a stated rate of 5% and which matures on 12/31. You receive £1,050, a *£50 yield for just 6 months*, for a 10% annual yield (100/1,000%).

Measuring Return with Yield
Yield is a figure that shows the *return* (not the interest) you get on a bond.
The simplest version of yield is calculated using the following formula:
Yield = coupon amount divided by price.
When you buy a bond at par, yield is equal to the interest rate.

Important note:
Bond prices and interest rates have an *inverse* relationship:
When the price of a bond rises, its interest rate falls and when the price falls, its interest rises.
When the price changes, so does the yield.

Example: If you buy a bond with a 10% coupon at its £1,000 par value, the yield is 10% (£100/£1,000)… Pretty simple stuff…
But if the *price goes down* to £800, then the *yield goes up* to 12.5% (£100/£800).
This happens because you are getting the same *guaranteed £100* on an asset that is worth £800.
Conversely, if the *bond goes up* in price to £1,200, *the yield shrinks* to 8.33% (*£100*/£1,200).

How can high yields and high prices both be good when they can't happen at the same time?
The answer depends on your point of view:

If you are a bond buyer, you want high yields. A buyer wants to pay £800 for the £1,000 bond, which gives the bond a high yield of 12.5%.
On the other hand, if you already own a bond, you've locked in your interest rate, so you hope the price of the bond goes up. This way you can cash out by selling your bond in the future.

Price "In the Market"
However, the factor that influences a bond more than any other is the level of prevailing interest rates in the economy:

- When *interest rates rise*, the *prices of bonds* in the market *fall*; thereby raising the yield of the older bonds and bringing them into line with newer bonds being issued with higher coupons.

- When *interest rates fall*, the *prices of bonds* in the market *rise*; thereby lowering the yield of the older bonds and bringing them into line with newer bonds being issued with lower coupons.

The shares

When you purchase stocks or equities/shares, you become a part-owner of the business.
This entitles you to vote at the shareholders' meeting and allows you to receive any profits that the company allocates to its owners.
These profits are referred to as *dividends*.

Share types:
A company may have as many different types of shares as it wishes, all with different conditions attached to them.
Generally share types are divided into the following categories:

- *Bearer shares*
  These shares are a legal instrument denoting company ownership and are usually in the form of share warrants.

- *Cumulative preference shares*
  These shares carry a right that, if the dividend cannot be paid in one year, it will be carried forward to successive years.

- *Preference shares*
  These shares normally carry a right that any annual dividends available for distribution will be paid preferentially on these shares before other classes.

- *Ordinary/common shares*
  As the name suggests these are the ordinary shares of the company with no special rights or restrictions.
  They may be divided into classes of different value.

- *Redeemable shares*

These shares are issued with an agreement that the company will buy them back at the option of the company or the shareholder after a certain period or on a fixed date.

A company cannot have redeemable shares only.

What are Shares outstanding?

They are common shares that have been authorised, issued and purchased by investors.

They have voting rights and represent ownership in the corporation by the person or institution that holds the shares.

What is a rights issue?

A rights issue is a way for a quoted company to raise money. Rather than take on debt, a quoted company can instead ask its shareholders to dig into their pockets to provide *extra* capital. The transaction involves the company giving *existing shareholders the right* to subscribe to newly issued shares *in proportion to their existing holdings*.

The *price* of the newly issued share *is fixed* and is *always set below the prevailing market price*.

As the name implies, the issue gives shareholders the *right* to buy the additional shares, but not the obligation.

The rights can be sold on to others who wish to take advantage of the offer and hence each right has a value.

A shareholder can take up all, some or none of the rights on offer.

What causes a rights issue?

They are not common corporate occurrences.

Usually the money is used for corporate expansion, a large takeover frequently being the main reason.

At the other end of the scale, *companies have used rights issue to save themselves from going bust or to increase their capital ratio (like during and just after the financial crisis 2007/2009 for example).*

What is Dilution of shares?
It is bad news for shareholders...
Their stake in a firm gets *watered down* when new shares are issued to fund a takeover deal or raise money.
In the case of a rights issue, shareholders are given the chance (*the right*) to buy more shares at a cheaper price.
If they don't buy, their shares are 'diluted' by the stock flooding the market
Stock/share dilution is a general term that results from the issue of *additional* common shares by a company.

A broader definition specifies dilution as any event that *reduces an investor's stock price below the initial purchase price.*
It is a *reduction in earnings per share* of common stock that occurs through the issuance of additional shares or the conversion of convertible securities.
Adding to the *number* of shares outstanding *reduces* the *value* of holdings of existing shareholders

How does the dilution work?
Example:
For simplicity, let's forget about the value of the holding before the rights issue and the subsequent subscription price.

- A company has 1000 shares in issue @ *£0.85*
Total value of shares in issue £850 (1000 x 0.85)
- The company organizes *a rights issue of 200 shares*.
So the total number of shares is now 1,200 and the value of one share is now: *£0.70833* (£850 divided by 1200)...

What happens to the share price of the company involved?
It depends.

This is the theory:
An investor holds 200 shares of RightsCo.
The market price of the share stands at 100p and the company then announces a "one for four" rights issue. The subscription price for the extra shares is set at 80p.
The value of the holding before the rights issue was:
200 shares at 100p = £200.00
To take up all the rights, the investor will have to purchase 50 new shares at a price of 80p, so the total amount of money that will pass from the investor to RightsCo is:
50 shares at 80p = £40.00
So, after the shares go ex-rights (usually a few weeks after the initial announcement and meaning that anyone buying them no longer has the right to buy the new shares) the share price, known as the ex-rights share price, will be:

$$\frac{\text{Total value of investment}}{\text{Total number of shares held}} = \frac{£200.00 + £40.00}{200 + 50} = 96\text{p}$$

Notes

- While bonds provide a steady stream of income, stocks are volatile… That is, they fluctuate in value on a daily basis. When you buy a stock, you are not guaranteed anything. Many stocks don't even pay dividends, in which case, the only way that you can make money is if the stock increases in value; which might not happen.

- You need to go through a broker/dealer to buy or sell shares, commodities, bonds etc … on any stock exchange or OTC … The same goes for spread betting and CFD.

The mutual funds

It is a *collection of stocks and bonds*.
When you buy a mutual fund, you *are pooling* your money with a number of other investors, which enables you (as part of a group) to pay a professional manager to select specific securities for you.
Mutual funds are all set up with a specific strategy in mind and their distinct focus can be nearly anything: large stocks, small stocks, bonds from governments, bonds from companies, stocks and bonds, stocks in certain industries, stocks in certain countries, etc.

The primary advantage of a mutual fund is that you can invest your money *without the time or the experience that are often needed to choose a sound investment.*

Theoretically, you should get a better return by giving your money to a professional than you would if you were to choose investments yourself. In reality, there are some aspects about mutual funds that you should be aware of before choosing them, but we won't discuss them here.

The commodities

Commodities are everything we grow, harvest or dig; such as: Oil, gold, silver, platinum, lead, copper, nickel, zinc, iron, sugar, coffee, soybean, corn, wheat, etc …
Note: We don't "harvest it" as such, but *carbon emissions* is regarded as a commodity (man-made greenhouse gas)…

There is another important class of *energy commodities* which includes electricity, gas, coal and crude oil.
Electricity has the particular characteristic that it is either *impossible or uneconomical to store*, hence, electricity must be consumed as soon as it is produced.
See electricity in appendix

Commodities are bought and sold on the *cash market* and they are traded on the *futures exchanges* in the form of *futures* contracts (derivatives).

Commodity prices are driven by *supply and demand.*
When a commodity is plentiful -- tomatoes in August, for example - prices are comparatively low.
When a commodity is scarce because of a bad crop or because it is out of season, the price will generally be higher.

You can buy *options* on many *commodity futures contracts* to participate in the market for less than it might cost you to buy the underlying futures contracts.
You can also invest through commodity

Note:
Most recently, financial products such as currency or stock and bond indexes have been called commodities …

Be careful …

When buying an option on sugar, the option is the *instrument/tool* to trade sugar (the *product*).

- A *commodity* is *not* a *financial product* as such; but is a general term for everything we grow, harvest or dig.
Gold, silver, platinum, lead, copper, nickel, zinc, iron, sugar, coffee, soybean, corn, wheat, cotton, oil and gas, etc …are *commodities*.

But an *option* to buy a commodity like sugar *(product)* is a *financial instrument* …

Note:
The word "derivative" (like the word "commodity") is a general term.

Examples of trading *derivatives*:
- You could either physically and directly buy sugar
    Or buy a sugar *option* (option being the derivative based on sugar).
    Or place a bet on the sugar price movement (*spread betting*)
- You could buy bonds
    Or you could *insure* these bonds against default (*Credit Default Swap)*

So you could have a derivative on a commodity *(commodity derivative):* An option on gold for example.

Let us now look at some complex financial instruments

THE DERIVATIVES

ISDA (International Swaps and Derivatives Association) is the trade organization of participants in the market for over-the-counter derivatives.

The name *"derivative"* is a general term; it's like the title of an enumeration …
A financial derivative product is *based on/derives* or takes its price *from* that of an underlying security such as an equity or commodity.
The derivative itself is merely a *contract between two parties*.

Its value is determined by fluctuations in the *underlying asset* like: Stocks, bonds, commodities, currencies, credit or default events, interest rates and market indexes.

Derivatives can be either *exchange-traded or traded "Over-The-Counter", with no clearing house...*

There are three major classes of derivatives products:

- *Options* (*based* on futures, securities or cash market).
- *Futures/Forwards* (*based* on commodities, bonds, financial indices or other securities).
- *Swaps* (Credit default swap, interest-rate swaps or equity swaps for example)

Some other derivatives are: Collateralised debt obligations, Warrants - *CFDs* (Contracts For Difference) - *Carbon credits* and *Spread betting.*

Notes

- The most important thing to remember about derivatives is *that most of them are not actual purchases*.
In most cases, the parties involved are only agreeing to make a *trade in the future*.
In the case of *options*, however, it is possible that the trade will not be completed after all.

- *Derivatives* are financial instruments which are used to *control risk* or paradoxically *exploit* risk.
Their use is commonplace in conventional banks, investment banks, insurance companies, pension funds, etc...

- Derivatives are usually broadly categorised by:

  The relationship between the underlying product and the derivative (e.g. forward, option, swap).

  The type of underlying (e.g. equity derivatives, foreign exchange derivatives, interest rate derivatives, commodity derivatives or credit derivatives).

  The market in which they trade (e.g. exchange-traded or over-the-counter).

- Another arbitrary distinction is between:
Vanilla derivatives (simple and more common) and *exotic* derivatives (more complicated and specialized)

- Derivatives are used by investors to:

  Provide *leverage or gearing.*

  Speculate and to make a profit if the value of the underlying asset moves the way they expect.

  Hedge or mitigate risk in the underlying product, by entering into a derivative contract whose value moves in the opposite direction to their underlying position and cancels part or all of it out.

An option

An option is a contract which gives the *buyer the right, but not the obligation* to buy or to sell an underlying asset *at a specific price* on or before a certain date and the *seller* the *obligation* to fulfil the contract.
The most important distinction is between the *Buyer* of a call or put option and its opposite, the *Seller* of an option (a call or a put):

As an option *buyer,* you *decide* whether to exercise the terms of the contract or not.
As an option *seller,* you *have to fulfil the obligations* of the contract.

Now, there are two types of *options* (for buyers and sellers): *CALL* option and *PUT* option.

PURCHASING a Call option
You have the *right to buy* (but *not* the obligation), but the *SELLER* has the obligation to sell the call.

PURCHASING a *Put* option
You have the *right* to *sell* (but *not* the obligation) – something you don't own (you borrow to short sell), but the *SELLER* has the obligation to honour the contract.

A *buyer* may *decide* to buy or sell – A *seller* has no choice…

Example of how it works:

Suppose you are buying a classic second-hand car.
You visit the owner, love the car and agree a price, but explain that you will not have the cash for 4 weeks.
The owner agrees to *hold the car and the price* for you for only 4 weeks, but on condition that you pay a small *non-refundable premium* for his trouble (this is in addition to the full price of the car).

Now let's assume that while you are waiting for the bank to supply the cash, the original factory where the cars were made is destroyed by fire…
Suddenly these cars *increase in value* sharply.
You, however, have a contract in writing at an agreed price, provided you buy within the next four weeks.

Now you, as the *buyer of the Call* or holder of the contract, have *two choices:*
a) You can exercise your contract by paying the seller the *agreed price* and immediately put the car on the market (if you want to) … and make a profit.
b) You can *sell your contract* on to someone else as it has now a higher premium value due to the *increase in value* of the underlying asset (the car).

Now, the *seller* of the car (the seller of the call/the writer of the contract option) has no idea who will exercise the contract, which could have been bought and sold many times over during the 4 week period; but *he will HAVE to deliver/to sell the asset at the price agreed;* It is a contract…

Selling Options

At this point, you might well ask, who sells the options that option buyers purchase?

The answer is that options are sold by other market participants known as option writers or grantors.

Their sole reason for writing options is to earn the premium paid by the option buyer.
If the option expires without being exercised *(which is what the option writer hopes will happen),* the writer retains the full amount of the premium.
If the option buyer exercises the option, however, the writer must pay the difference between the market value and the exercise price.

It should be emphasized that unlike an option buyer who has a limited risk (the loss of the option premium), the writer of an option has unlimited risk.
This is because any gain realized by the option buyer if and when he exercises the option will become a loss for the option writer.

Futures contracts

The contracts are traded on a Futures exchange.

Whether you are dealing in orange juice, wheat, silver or gold, if you are investing in commodities, you are dealing in the *futures market.*
The goal is to make money when that commodity either gains or loses in value.
Note:
In many cases, the *underlying asset to a futures contract* may not be traditional "commodities" at all – the underlying asset can be currencies, securities or financial instruments such as stock indexes and interest rates.

In essence, you are betting on the future of the commodity.
Futures are an agreement to buy or sell a set amount of a commodity or financial instrument at a set price in the future.

The price is agreed on by the buyer and seller and included in a contract.
The investor is required to make only a small deposit to control a much greater amount of the commodity.
The small deposit, typically around 10 percent, is called a *margin payment.*
Therefore, if you wish to control 100 ounces of gold and gold on that day is worth £350 per ounce or a total of £35,000, you could control the entire 100 ounces of gold by putting down a £3,500 margin payment.
If the price of gold rises, you will be credited the difference, but if the price drops, you will be responsible for coming up with additional margin capital to control the 100 ounces of gold.
In essence you are responsible for the entire £35,000 worth of gold.

The idea of controlling a much larger amount of goods, with a margin payment, makes futures both an exciting and a very risky investment.

Note:
The main fundamental differences between options and futures are:

- An *option* gives the buyer the right, but *not the obligation* to buy (or sell) a certain asset at a specific price at any time during the life of the contract and the seller the obligation to fulfil the contract.

- A *futures* contract gives the buyer and the seller the *obligation* to fulfil the contract of that asset at a specific future date and at agreed price, unless the holder's position is closed prior to expiration (the contract is sold to someone else).

Apart from commissions, an investor can enter into a futures contract with no upfront cost whereas buying an options position does require the payment of *a premium*.
The premium is the maximum that a purchaser of an option can lose.

Forward contracts

Fundamentally, forward and futures contracts have the *same* function:
Both types of contracts allow people to buy or sell a specific type of asset at a specific time at a given price.

However, it is in the *specific details* that these contracts differ:

- First of all, *futures contracts* are *exchange-traded* and therefore, are standardised contracts.
- *Forward contracts*, on the other hand, are *private agreements* between two parties and are not as rigid in their stated terms and conditions.
Because forward contracts are private agreements, there is always a chance that a party may default on its side of the agreement.
- *Futures contracts* have *clearing houses that guarantee the transactions,* which drastically lowers the probability of default to almost never.

- Secondly, for forward contracts, settlement of the contract occurs at the end of the contract whereas futures contracts are *marked-to-market daily*, which means that daily changes are settled day by day until the end of the contract.
- Furthermore, settlement for *futures contracts* can occur over a range of dates.
Forward contracts, on the other hand, only possess one settlement date.

SWAPs

Swaps are contracts to *exchange* cash on or before a specified future date, based on the underlying value of currencies/exchange rates, bonds/interest rates, commodities, stocks or other assets; the parties *"swap"* the cash flow streams.

While swaps are used for various purposes - from hedging to speculation - their fundamental purpose is to change the character of an asset or liability *without liquidating* that asset or liability.
For example:
An investor realising returns from an equity investment, can swap those returns into less risky fixed income cash flows; *without having to liquidate the equities.*

Swap spread
In finance, *swap spread* is a popular way to indicate the credit spreads in a market.
It is the difference (positive) between swap rates and the relevant government bond market.

For example, if the fixed-rate of a 5-year swap is 7.26% and the 5-year Treasury is yielding at 6.43%, the swap spread is 7.26% - 6.43% = 83 bps.

See appendix for more details about SWAP

Credit Default SWAP - CDS *(swap the risk of defaulting).*

CDSs are the largest credit derivative products and are traded over the counter. It is a sort of *insurance.*

They are designed *to transfer credit risk from one party to another.* By creating or eliminating credit exposures, they allow institutions to more *effectively manage credit risks.*

The *buyer* of a credit default swap *pays a premium* for effectively *insuring against a debt default.*
He receives a lump sum payment if the debt instrument is defaulted.
The *seller* of a credit default swap *receives monthly payments* from the buyer.
If the debt instrument defaults they have to pay the agreed amount to the buyer of the credit default swap.

Example of Credit Default Swap
An investment trust owns £1 million corporation bonds issued by a private housing firm.
If there is a risk the private housing firm may default on repayments, the investment trust may *buy a CDS* (an insurance) from a hedge fund. The CDS is worth £1 million.
The investment trust will pay *an interest* on this credit default swap of say 3% (£30,000 a year for the duration of the contract).
If the private housing firm *doesn't default*, the hedge fund gains the interest from the investment bank and pays nothing out. *It is simple profit.*
If the private housing firm *does default*, then the hedge fund has to *pay compensation* to the investment bank of £1 million - the value of the credit default swap.

Therefore the hedge fund takes on a larger risk and could end up paying £1million

Why would people buy Credit Default Swaps?

1. Hedge against risk

- Suppose an investment fund manager owns mortgage bonds from riskymortgage.co.uk.

It might be worried about losing all its investment…

Therefore, to *hedge* against the risk of default, he could purchase a credit default swap from an insurance company.

If riskymortgage.co.uk defaulted, the manager would lose his investment, but receive a payoff from the insurance company to compensate.

However, if there was no default, the fund manager would lose the premium paid to the insurance company…

2. Speculation

- Suppose a hedge fund felt realemortgage.co was very likely to default because of a rise in home repossessions.

They would buy a credit default swap.

If the debt was defaulted, then they would make profit from Lloyds TSB.

Clearly the more risky a bond is the higher premium will be required from a buyer of a credit default swap.

3. Arbitrage

- If a company's financial position improves, the credit rating should also improve and therefore, the CDS spread should *fall* to reflect improved rating.

This makes CDS more attractive to *sell CDS protection.* If the company position deteriorated, CDS protection would be more attractive to *buy.*

Naked CDSs

You don't have to actually own debt to take/buy a credit default swap. This is *naked* speculation ...

The buyer has no stake in the underlying asset being insured against default...

But why should a hedge fund be allowed to insure itself against Paris defaulting on its national debt if the fund does not own French bonds?

It creates an obvious temptation to spread malicious rumours in order to turn it into a one-way bet ...

Credit Default Swaps in Markets

The size of the credit default market dwarfs that of the stock market and the bond market they represent.

Therefore, this shows that credit default swaps are being used for speculation and not insuring against actual bonds...

Credit Default Swaps are unregulated and because they get traded so frequently there is uncertainty of who owns them and whether the holders can actually pay *in the event of a negative credit event...* (AIG could not and had to be bailed out...).

It's estimated that the global *credit default swaps market is now worth around $65 trillion* (close to the annual GDP of the entire planet).

However, CDSs serve a very valuable function by allowing companies to transfer credit risk efficiently.

Collateralised Debt Obligations (CDOs)

These *credit derivatives* are complex financial tools that *re-package* individual loans *into a product* that can be sold on the secondary market to investors.
These packages consist of auto loans, credit card debts, mortgage bonds or corporate debts and are sold as *safe or risky investments* (depending of the underlying assets).

CDO's were created to provide more liquidity in the economy. It allows banks and corporations *to sell off debt*, which frees up more capital to invest and reduce the amount of debt on their balance sheet.

One way to think of them is like this:
A bank may have some mortgage loans (prime and sub-prime mortgages) which are worth £10,000.
This bank re-packages these loans as mortgage bonds and may sell them as CDO to another bank.
As the mortgage is paid back, the second bank will get interest payments.
However, if people default on their mortgages, then the person owning the CDO is going to see a decline in the value of the CDO.
The first bank has in effect *sold on* its mortgage loans to another company.
Therefore, if the person with a mortgage defaults, the risk is born by the person who bought the CDO.

The owner of a CDO usually buys an "insurance" called Credit Default Swap (CDS), in case of a payment default.

Note – **CDOs and CDSs**

For a better understanding, this note should be read in conjunction with "Financial crisis" in Appendix

Note
These two derivatives played an important role during the financial crisis (2007/2009) because when mortgage defaults rose significantly, many banks, insurance companies and other financial institutions (together with some rich individuals) around the world went bankrupt…or had to be bailed out (and a few became much richer)…

… Many institutional investors and speculators had bought millions worth of sub-prime mortgage bonds CDOs; but even if they were "CDS-insured", the bodies (banks, insurance companies and other financial institutions) that sold these "CDSs insurances", were unable to fulfil their obligations (pay out on their policy when things went wrong)…
They did not have *sufficient assets in reserve* and *too many borrowers defaulted.*

Consequently many of them went bust or had to be rescued by their respective government (AIG, for example)…

In the USA, of the more than $500bn of backed asset-securities CDOs sold in the boom years, $50bn have experienced an "event of default"…

At the same time, many hedge funds made billions by betting *against* risky CDOs, devised by banks, linked to the housing market (mortgage bonds) and sold to financial investors (by shorting the CDOs and buying CDSs)…

Carbon credit *or Certified Emission Reduction unit*

Carbon emission is a sort of "commodity" (man-made greenhouse gas) and a *carbon credit* is its *derivative* ...

Main body
United Nations Framework Convention on Climate Change

The *Kyoto Protocol* has created a mechanism under which countries (not the USA) that have been emitting more carbon and other gases (greenhouse gases include ozone, carbon dioxide, methane, nitrous oxide and even water vapour) have *voluntarily* decided that they will reduce the use of fossil fuels and bring down the level of carbon they are emitting to the levels of early 1990s.

It is supposed to encourage companies to invest in low-polluting technologies by forcing them to buy allowances to cover their emissions.
Efficient companies can profit by selling their unused allowances.

A *carbon credit (or permit)* is created when the *equivalent* of one metric tonne of carbon dioxide-equivalent (greenhouse gases) is prevented from entering the atmosphere.

Carbon offsetting is the process by which a successful emission reduction is produced in one geographical location and claimed by another.

Carbon emissions trading (or cap & trade).
It is a fully fungible (trade-able) financial instrument.

You can compare the *carbon trading system* (CTS) to a bank; as you can transfer allowances from account to account.
The trading scheme limits the carbon emissions of all big EU factories by issuing them with allowances or permits (credits) for each tonne of carbon emitted, which companies can trade for themselves.

Carbon credits can be traded privately, over the counter or on the spot markets such as France's BlueNext (European Climate Exchange), like any stock.

Climate exchanges provide a *spot market, futures and options* market.
They are mostly purchased by governments and corporations who have a legal or moral duty to reduce their carbon footprint.
Some individuals are also purchasing sufficient personal carbon credits to claim a 'carbon neutral' lifestyle.
Carbon prices are normally quoted in euros per tonne of CO2 (15 euros in 2011).

Carbon Credit Certification
Every project looking to *earn carbon credits*, be it wind, solar, reforestation or any other carbon emissions reduction strategy has to go through a strict and rigorous third party validation and certification to make sure the project can justify and quantify the amount if CO2 it intends to reduce.

A commercially independent *Green Investment Bank* (to help fund the shift to a low-carbon economy is being set up by the government).

Climate change targets are getting tough …
Every company and one day every household will have to control their CO_2 emissions…
Europe is already committed to slashing CO_2 emissions by 20% and EU talks of 30% cut in carbon dioxide emissions across Europe by 2020 …
This higher target would put more pressure on the UK to switch from coal, gas and oil power stations to "green" energy such as wind farms.

For information - *Wind farms*:
Most of the extra electricity would come from offshore wind, adding another 2,500 wind turbines to the 7,000 already planned in the UK for the next decade.
Britain is already committed to cutting its CO_2 emissions by 34% over the next decade.
This is because emissions in Britain are higher (only 10% of electricity is currently coming from renewables) and Britain needs to do more …

Note:
- It is said that carbon will be the world's biggest commodity market …

Now let us look at two important back-office activities

CLEARING & SETTLEMENT

It is the process of matching, registering and guaranteeing transactions.

- *Clearing*

In banking and finance, clearing denotes all activities from the time a commitment is made for a transaction until it is settled.

Clearing House

A clearing house ensures that trades between a buyer and a seller are completed; *even if one party fails to pay …*

A clearing house (like Eurex and NYSE Liffe) holds all deposits and margin requirements of the clearing participants who have to cover their commitments with the Clearing House on a day to day basis.

Clearing houses spread the risk of default of a counter-party because their members share the costs.

Note: OTC transactions do not go through an exchange or a clearing house, like the trading of derivatives for example.

Settlement

It is the effective transfer of ownership of securities from a seller to a buyer and the transfer of cash from a buyer to a seller.

Clearing and settlement are important "back-office" post-trade activities.

Note: Events have shown that big financial institutions can disappear overnight and so the primary role of central counter-parties (CCPs) in terms of guaranteeing trades should not be overlooked.

COUNTER-PARTY
&
CENTRAL COUNTER-PARTY

The (2007/2009) crisis has highlighted the necessity of having central counter-parties in order to mitigate the risk of trading.

A *counter-party* is a party with which a transaction is done.
If A sells something to B, then B is a counter-party from A's point of view and vice-versa.
The risk that the counter-party will fail to fulfil its obligations - usually either by failing to pay or by failing to deliver securities - is called *counter-party risk.*
There are a number of ways of controlling counter-party risk. Some are trading mechanisms such as DVP (delivery versus payment) or the use of a *central* counter-party.

A *central counter-party* is a financial institution that acts as an intermediary between security market participants.
This reduces the amount of counter-party risk that market participants are exposed to.
Trades on most major stock exchanges (including London) go through a central counter-party.
The seller of a security sells to the central counter-party. The central counter-party simultaneously sells to the buyer.
This means that if one party defaults then the central counter-party will absorb the loss.
This eliminates both the risk of direct financial loss through a default and the risk of indirect loss through having to unwind a trade.
It is therefore a more complete method of reducing counter-party risk than alternatives such as simple DVP

LAW INFORCEMENT
RULES and REGULATIONS

- *Tri-partite:*
To regulate the economy and maintain financial stability, a *tri-partite regulatory* structure had been created in 1997, when the then chancellor, made the *Bank of England independent* (from the government). It included:
The Bank of England - The Treasury - The FSA (Financial Services Authority)
Author's note: Everybody and nobody was really in charge; as nobody had an overall responsibility ...

One of the most important regulator bodies
- The *Financial Reporting Council* (FRC)
It is the independent regulator responsible for promoting high quality corporate governance and reporting to foster investment.
It sets and enforces accounting and auditing standards.

Not to forget the law enforcement bodies ...
- The *Serious Fraud Office* is a government department and is part of the UK criminal justice system.
Its aim is to protect society by pursuing and prosecuting those who commit serious and complex fraud.
- The *City of London Police* is the territorial police force responsible for law-enforcement within the City of London.
It is responsible for co-coordinating Operation Archway, the national intelligence reporting system for mass share-marketing fraud (called boiler room).

- Other agencies: Trading Standards services, the Office of Fair Trading and the Serious Organized Crime Agency.

New rules and regulations for England and Wales

In 2010, to avoid a repeat of the financial crisis (2007/2009), new rules, regulations and new bodies/agencies have been created by the new coalition government:

First, *the tri-partite as such was abolished* and then:

- An *Office for Budget Responsibility* was created. It is an official but "independent" *forecast* for *economic growth and public borrowing*
- A *Financial Policy Committee* (charged with maintaining financial stability) was also created.

The FSA will be *abolished* by 2012 and will be replaced by:

- A *Prudential Regulatory Authority*
- A *Consumer Protection and Markets Authority agency*
- An E*conomic Crime Agency*.

Remuneration:
Pay practices are being curbed at banks and hedge funds (for senior managers and people designated as risk takers):

- No more than 50% of the reward can be paid in cash.
- At least 40% of a bonus must be in *deferred shares* for several years.
- Introduction of a *claw back* policy.
- Abolition of *guaranteed* pay deals

Tax:
A permanent *levy* on big banks profits has been created together with a new *tax on financial trading*.

Bribery Act:
A new act has been introduced (from April 2011).

At European level:

- *Bank stress tests* (to prove that a bank has sufficient capital to cope with economic growth scenarios) have been implemented.

- From January 2011, three pan-European banking "super-watchdogs" (financial regulators) have been created.

  The *European Banking Authority* is based in London.

  The *European Securities and Markets Authority* is based in Paris.

  The *European Insurance Occupational Pensions Authority is* based in Frankfurt.

  Moreover, the *European Systematic Risk Board* (an agency of the European Central Bank is also based in Frankfurt).

- *Sovereign debt crisis/bailing out of states*

A *European safety net* has been created; it consists of:

  The European Financial Stability Mechanism (EFSM), available to all 27 EU members - which can lend up to 60 bn euros.

  The European Financial Stability Facility (fund) (EFSF), available to only the 16 countries of the Eurozone - which is backed by 440 bn euros worth of Eurozone government guarantees.

  Moreover, the International Monetary fund (IMF) might lend up to 50% of what Europe may provide…

World-wide new regulations - Basel III Accords
(Basel is a Swiss city) - 12 September 2010 -

The *Basel Committee on Banking Supervision* has decreed that tougher *capital standards* are necessary to prevent another financial crisis...
More *capital* and *liquidity* must be kept in reserve, as a back up...

So regulators from around the world agreed on a new rule book:

- Banks will have to hold *high-quality capital.*
- Basel III Accords set a new core *Tier 1 capital ratio of 4.5 %* plus a new capital "*conservation buffer" of a further 2.5%,* phased in from 2016.
  So in effect the rule sets a floor of *7%.*
- Banks whose *capital falls within the buffet zone* will face *restrictions on paying dividends, share buybacks and discretionary bonuses.*

The new rules will be phased in from January 2013 when the core Tier 1 will rise from the present 2% to 3.5% and so on...
The Basel Committee also announced a *liquidity ratio.*
The regulators set a six year transition period that will conclude at the end of 2018.

Note: Davos World Economic Forum - January 2011 – Regulators are asking for more capital to be put aside; some advocate up to 20% of capital ratio...

Author's note: As a consequence, banks will have *less capital* to trade and will have to keep some of their profit (to build up their capital), the cost of borrowing will rise and returns on capital for investors will diminish...

Other proposed laws/regulations:

- European regulators could have the *power to write down bank debt and force governments' bondholders to bail out lenders…*
(The holders of the senior debt of the banks should be forced to take a hair cut or convert debt into equity if the bank does not have enough money …).
It would mean that senior bondholders, as well as shareholders, could see their investment wiped out in the event of a bankruptcy.

- *National deposit guarantee schemes (funded by the banking industry) to pay for the cost of winding up a failing bank.*

- *New legislation on derivatives and short-selling* could come into effect by 2012:
To reduce counter-party risk (and for more transparency), derivatives traders would have to use *clearing houses.*
Traders would have to *disclose short-selling positions* to regulators if they exceed a certain percentage (of a company issued capital).
A ban or tighter controls for "naked" short-selling

Note: About short-selling
However let us *not ignore the valuable service provided in the early discovery of overvalued stock...*

- Another law may regulate credit default swaps (CDSs) which allow traders to insure against a borrower defaulting.

- Furthermore, as an extra safeguard, a mandatory *leverage (borrowing) ratio* will be introduced in January 2018.

- A European *credit rating body may be created.*

- The "*breaking-up*" of banks (too big to fail) is a possibility.

- Absolute return funds

Absolute return funds work differently to conventional "relative return" funds, where the manager competes against a benchmark such as the FTSE All-Share index.

Traditional fund managers can claim success even if their fund falls, provided their benchmark falls further.

But Absolute return fund managers are expected to produce positive returns even in stormy markets.

- Alpha

Alpha is one of the two measures (the other is *beta*) traditionally used to judge the performance of a money manager.

It refers to the *excess return* that a money manager can generate by using his skills to pick the best performing stocks in the financial markets.

If he generates a positive alpha, this means they have made a *higher return than a benchmark index*, such as the S&P 500.

If you beat the index by 0.8%, then you have achieved an alpha of 0.8.

On the other hand, a manager who has missed the market's return by 0.6% would have an alpha of -0.6.

Note:

Alpha is also a technical risk ratio.

When returns are calculated, it takes into account the amount of *capital put at risk* by investors.

For example, one manager risks £100m and generates a return of £200m.

This might look impressive on a balance sheet, but it is a riskier strategy than that of a manager who risked £2m but generated a return of £10m.

- Analyses

For an investor, there are two types of analysis to predict price movements.

They are: *Technical* analysis and *fundamental* analysis …

a) *Technical analysis* is a method of *evaluating securities* by analysing statistics generated by market activity, such as *prices* and *volume* (daily number of shares of a security that change hands between a buyer and a seller).

Charts are often used as *a tool* to show patterns that can suggest future trends. It is based on how price movements have performed historically.

b) *Fundamental analysis* is a method of *judging a company's financials and operations.*

A company's fundamental data is directly related to the company's performance, as opposed to statistical data, which is used in technical analysis.

As the term suggests, you have to analyze the "fundamentals" such as:

The company's cash flow profile - How the company operates - The debts and assets on its balance sheet - The management's investment strategy…

Two of the most popular yardsticks that investors use are a company's *Earnings Per Share (EPS)* and *Price-to-Earnings ratio (P/E):*

- *EPS* is the total *earnings* divided by the company's *number of shares.*

It is a measure of how expensive the company's shares are for every £1 profit it makes.

- *P/E* is calculated by dividing the *share price* by the company's full year total *EPS.*

In 2010, the average P/E multiple for UK stocks is 13%

However, it is only meaningful when you compare it against the *average* P/E in the *sector it belongs to* or against the P/E ratio of a competitor.

Compare apples with apples...

> - If you use the latest *full year EPS* in your calculations then you are looking at the *historic P/E.*
> - If you use the *forecast earnings* per share, then you are looking at its *prospective or forward P/E.*

As a rule of thumb, the higher the P/E ratio, the more expensive the company's shares are and the lower the P/E the cheaper they are.

If for example Toco company has a P/E ratio of 15 while Bury company has a P/E ratio of 11, you could say that Toco company is *overvalued* relative to Bury company... or Bury is *undervalued* relative to Toco.

Note: Companies with a very high or very low P/E should be treated with caution...

- Arbitrage
It is the simultaneous buying and selling of securities in different markets with the purpose of profiting from the price difference in the markets.

A person who engages in arbitrage is called an arbitrageur -
It is the practice of taking advantage of a price differential between two or more markets.

Arbitrage is not simply the act of buying a product in one market and selling it in another for a higher price at some later time...

The transactions must occur *simultaneously* to avoid exposure to market risk or the risk that prices may change on one market before both transactions are complete.
See Risk and Merger arbitrage further down

Note
Arbitrage can only be done profitably with computers examining a large number of prices and automatically exercising a trade when the prices are far enough out of balance.

- Assets Return
Where *asset turnover* tells an investor the *total sales* for each £1 of assets, *assets return* tells an investor how much *profit* a company generated for each £1 *in assets*.

The *return on assets figure* is *a sure-fire way* to gauge the *asset intensity* of a business.
Companies such as telecommunication providers, car manufacturers and railroads are *very asset-intensive*, meaning they require big, expensive machinery or equipment to generate a profit.
Advertising agencies and software companies, on the other hand, are generally *very asset-light* (in the case of a software companies, once a program has been developed, employees simply copy it to a 5p disk, throw a manual in and mail it out to stores).

Assets Return measures a company's earnings *in relation to all of the resources it had at its disposal* (the shareholders' capital plus short and long-term borrowed funds).
Thus, it is the most stringent and excessive test of return to shareholders.
If a company has no debt, the *return on assets* and *return on equity* figures will be the same.

The lower the profit per pound of assets, the more asset-intensive a business is.
The higher the profit per pound of assets, the less asset-intensive a business is.

- **Auction market** - An important job for market-makers
The auction market *determines the price* you pay for a security when you buy it from a broker on an exchange or directly from an exchange yourself.
The auction system is also used by stock markets – such as the London Stock Exchange – to formulate prices at the start of each trading day.

A price for an asset is generated when buyers submit competing bids and sellers competing offers all at the same time.
As you might expect, the highest bid offered for the asset determines the price that it will be sold for.

The auction market is essential for generating prices because one cannot perform a transaction *in secret* on a mainstream exchange.
However in an OTC transaction, the buyer and seller will negotiate the price of an asset between themselves.

- **Backwardation/Contango**
Backwardation is a market condition where spot prices exceed forward prices.
Contango is the opposite condition, where forward prices exceed spot prices.

The terms are most commonly used in oil markets but are also applied in certain commodity and energy markets.
In oil markets, the prevailing condition may reflect immediate supply and demand.

If crude oil is *contango*, it may indicate immediately available supply.
Backwardation can indicate an immediate shortage.

- Bank *company*
A bank company is defined as the business entity or group that actually owns one or more banks, but does not necessarily engage in banking itself.

- Bank covenant
It is an *agreement/contract* between an individual or a company taking out a *bank loan* and the *bank* granting the loan. The *covenant* outlines the conditions upon which the loan is granted...
Breach of covenant (can't meet the commitments).

- Bankruptcy – Receivership - Liquidation - Administration
(See pre-pack administration further down).
In most countries there *are two tests for bankruptcy*:

a) A company that *cannot pay its debts* because there is *not enough money* in the bank
b) A company with *liabilities* (or what it owes) that *exceed its assets* (such as property, inventory or what it is owed).

In the UK or in Europe, the first scenario would usually tip a company into *liquidation* unless it was rescued.
Under the second scenario, which is sometimes called balance sheet insolvency, the company is more likely to avoid liquidation *by negotiating with its creditors*.

Confusingly, *UK firms* will *not* go *bankrupt* at all - here the term is reserved for *personal* bankruptcies.
Companies *running out of money* instead enter a *Company Voluntary Arrangement* (CVA), go into *administration* or *receivership* or are *wound up*.

Notes

- *Bankruptcy in the US is different*
In the *US* it is more common for a company to go into *Chapter 11 bankruptcy*, which gives it an opportunity to re-organise and emerge from bankruptcy.
- *France* has a system called *Judicial Composition*, similar to Chapter 11, but only about 7% of bankrupt companies go down this route.

What happens when a company falls into liquidation?

A company is liquidated when the situation is hopeless and there is no plan to rescue it.
At this point an insolvency agent takes over the company from its management, sells the assets and returns any money to its creditors (*preferential* creditors).
Shareholders have no hope of recovering any of their investment.

What is the difference between going into administration and going into receivership?

In the UK, the banks that have lent money on a secured basis have the right to call in a *receiver* to sort out the assets and look after their interests.
Under new reforms, the UK plans to move away from the receivership system to the *administration* model favoured by Continental Europe.

For information

Personal insolvency:
From 07 April 2009, a new ultra-fast bankruptcy is available to debtors and is expected to trigger a 20% surge in the number of *personal insolvencies* … (not company insolvency).

Debt Relief Orders will allow someone with little or no income to ask the Official Receiver to write off their borrowings.

After 12 months they will be discharged and able to start afresh…

- Basel I - Basel II and Basel III Committee Accords
It refers to the banking supervision Accords (recommendations on banking laws and regulations) by the *Basel committee* (international banking regulator).

The purpose of these accords, which were initially published in June 2004, was to create an international standard that banking regulators could use when creating regulations about how much *capital* banks need to put aside to guard against the types of financial and operational risks banks face.

Capital/debt or risk ratio …
Generally speaking, these rules mean that the greater risk to which the bank is exposed, the greater the amount of capital the bank needs to hold to safeguard its solvency and overall economic stability.
See *Tier 1 and 2 capital* further down…

12 September 2010
The *endorsement of the Basel III* reform was the cornerstone of the world's response to the financial crisis (2007/2009).
See Basel III Accords further down

- Bellwether

A bellwether is a castrated ram (a sheep that leads the herd often wearing a bell).

In business and finance, a bellwether is any entity in a given arena that serves to create or influence trends or to presage future happenings.

The term has come to mean something that is a leading indicator of a trend

- Beta

Beta is the correlation between a stock and an index.

Beta is a mesure of *stock volatility* and reflects the degree to which its price fluctuates relative to the overall market.

It effectively gives investors an idea of *how risky* a stock is compared to the wider index.

If a company has a beta value of one, then its share price ought to move in line with the market.

A beta value of less than one, indicates that the share price is less volatile than the benchmark, while a value greater than one signals a relatively volatile stock.

See Alpha

- Boiler room (fraud)

It involves fraudsters using high pressure sales tactics to “con” investors into buying non-tradable, over-priced or even non-existent shares.

- Broad money

It is the widest measurement of the money supply (the total amount of money available in an economy at a particular point in time).

The different types of money are typically classified as Ms. The number of Ms usually ranges from M0 (narrowest) to M3 (broadest).

For example, M0 is for: Notes and coins (currency) in circulation and in bank vaults, plus reserves which commercial banks hold in their accounts with the central bank.

- Broker/dealer

A broker dealer is a person or an organisation (bank) that trades securities for its own account or on behalf of its customers.

An investment bank is a broker dealer.

A *broker* executes trade orders on behalf of a customer.

A *dealer* executes trades for its own account.

Note: Nobody can buy/sell shares, bonds, commodities, derivatives, etc by themselves ... They must go through a broker dealer; let it be trade on a stock exchange or over the counter.

- Burn rate

It is the rate at which a new company uses up its venture capital to finance overhead *before* generating positive cash flow from operations.

Burn rate is usually quoted in terms of *cash spent per month.*

- Cable (Forex)

Slang used among forex traders referring to the exchange rate between the U.S. dollar and the British pound sterling.

Because it is the norm in forex for most major currencies to be quoted against the U.S. dollar on a regular basis, "cable" is a commonly used term.

The origins of this term are attributed to the fact that in the 1800s, the dollar/pound sterling exchange rate was transmitted via transatlantic cable.

Forex brokers are sometimes referred to as "cable dealers".

"Cable" can also be used to refer simply to the British pound sterling.

- **Capex** (short for capital expenditures)
Capex are expenditures creating *future benefits*. It is an investment.

- **Carry trade**
The carry trade is the practice of borrowing in low interest currencies (normally the yen) and then using the money to buy high-yielding assets, such as commodities, equities or bonds; often denominated in a different currency with higher interest rates.

Example
A trader borrows 1,000 Japanese yen from a Japanese bank, converts the funds into U.S. dollars and buys a bond for the equivalent amount.
Let's assume that the bond pays 4.5% and the Japanese interest rate (on 1,000 yen) is set at 2%.
The trader stands to make a profit of 2.5%; as long as the exchange rate between the countries does not change.

- **Chinese wall**
In business, it is a firewall (a barrier) implemented within a company to separate and isolate persons who make investment decisions from persons who are privy to undisclosed material information which may influence those decisions.
This is a way of avoiding conflict of interests.

- **Compounding**
Compounding occurs when your investment *earnings* or savings account *interests* are *added to your principal.*
As your investment base gets larger, it has the potential to grow faster. The longer your money is invested, the more you stand to gain from compounding.
For example, if you invested £10,000 earning 8% annually and reinvested all your earnings, you would have £21,589 in your account after 10 years.

If instead of reinvesting you withdrew the earnings each year, you would have collected £800 a year or £8,000 over the 10 years. The £3,589 difference is the benefit of 10 years of compound growth.

- Contango/ Backwardation

Contango is a market condition where forward prices exceed spot prices.
Backwardation is the opposite condition where spot prices exceed forward prices.

- Contingent convertible bonds (cocos)

They are bonds that turn into equity in time of stress.
See bonds in the first part of this manual.

- Contract For Difference (CFD) – A derivative

Basically, you can physically buy and sell equities/shares, bonds, commodities, currencies, etc … on a stock exchange (or over the counter); but to do that, you will need 100% of the money (to buy) and will have to pay capital gain tax and stamp duty … (furthermore you'll be "stuck" with your buy…).

However, an alternative way of trading is via derivatives such as *Contracts for Difference*.
They offer all the benefits of trading shares without having to physically own them (you borrow them from or through a broker/investment bank …)

A CFD is a contract between two parties to exchange the *difference in value* of a particular share or index between the time at which a contract is opened and the time at which it is closed.
It is exactly like physically trading the stock market; except that you *only need a small amount of money up front.*
This is known as your CFD *margin* (you borrow the difference from the broker).

There are generally two types of CFDs:
CFDs offered by a *Market Maker* and CFDs offered via *Direct Market Access* with each having its benefits.

- *Market Maker* (see definition)
  Market Maker CFDs are not directly hedged ("secured/insured") in the underlying physical market; instead it *remains the discretion* of a dealer or market marker as to whether they hedge CFD position in the underlying market.
  So the provider can be exposed to a significant amount of market risk.

- *Direct Market Access* (DMA)
  Direct Market Access CFDs result in an order being passed *directly through* to the underlying physical market with no dealer or market maker intervention, resulting in real time execution and true market prices.
  Note: Together with the use of the *Level 2 data* (real time extra information available on electronic platform), it may help make the difference between a winning and a losing trading plan (rather than just working with a market maker).

Contract for Difference and hedging
A firm is *unlikely* to enter into a large CFD transaction with a client without hedging most if not all of the position in the underlying cash market.
In other words, although they are technically the counter-party to the client, the *relationship* is effectively *the private investor buying from the institution.*
The price at which the CFD is booked is always the same as the hedge, which you will see *simultaneously* in the real or 'cash' market, where equities are exchanged for cash.

Hedging indices
See "hedging" and "short-selling" in the "Jargon" section -

Market makers/brokers cannot "borrow" indices to hedge; so they will normally cover themselves by buying/selling *index Futures* which are traded on various exchanges.

There are concerns that CFDs are being used to *secretly* accumulate large stakes in companies, as a result of *hush-hush agreements* between dealers and CFD investors…

Danger!
These agreements involve the dealer promising *to sell* the shares (which *he has purchased to hedge its exposure* from the sale of the CFD) on to the investor, once the contract expires…
These informal side agreements may offer investors a back door *to taking over a company…*
Do not forget that to start with, as a CFD buyer, in real terms, (officially) the client *does not buy* the underlying product …

- CPI
CPI is the *consumer* price index (**RPI** is the *retail* price index).

- Credit rating agency

A credit rating agency is a company that assigns credit ratings for issuers of certain types of debts as well as the debt instruments themselves.

A credit rating for an issuer takes into consideration the issuer's credit worthiness (i.e. *its ability to pay back a loan*) and affects the interest rate applied to the particular security being issued.

AAA+ being the highest rating for a debt and the risk of default is "practically nil"…

Credit ratings are used by investors, issuers, investment banks, broker/dealers and governments.
These agencies can rate individual products like a bond or a gilt, companies, banks and governments.
For investors, credit rating agencies provide "independent" (they make their money by charging issuer fees), easy-to-use measurements of relative *credit risk.*

However, in some cases, agencies have potential conflict of interests ...
"Downgrades" can have huge de-stabilizing effect ...
Over-reliance on credit ratings played a key role in the financial crisis (2007/2009)...

Three of the best known agencies are Standard & Poor, Moody's and Fitch.

Note
Europe and USA are talking about creating their own sovereign and independent *credit rating* body ...

For information
In contrast to Credit rating agency, a company that issues *credit scores* for *individual* credit-worthiness is generally called a *credit bureau.*

- **"Dark pool"** trading
They are electronic trading platforms that offer anonymous trading away from stock exchanges.
It is a facility which allows big blocks of shares to be traded at prices which are not posted *until after* the trade.

- Davos
World Economic Forum held in the picturesque town of Davos in the Swiss Alps.

- Debenture
Debenture is the traditional name given to a loan agreement where the borrower is a company.

- Distressed debt
Debt with low junk status and a market price substantially below par value.

Investors sometimes buy distressed debt on the possibility that management can renegotiate loan agreements and keep the issuer out of bankruptcy.
Alternatively, distressed debt may offer potential value in the event the issuer is liquidated.

- **"Dry powder"** (Informal/slang)
It is a term for cash reserves, especially to cover unforeseen, future obligations.

- EBT – Earnings Before Tax

- EBITDA – Earnings Before Interest, Taxes, Depreciation and Amortisation is also called *Operating profit.*
It represents cash available (to pay creditors in case of liquidation for example).

- Economy
An economy is a system of *production*, *distribution* and *consumption.*

It refers also to the measure of how a country or region is progressing in terms of product.
GDP (Gross Domestic Product), is one of the ways of measuring the size of its economy.

The GDP of a country is defined as the total market value of all final goods and services produced within a country in a given period of time (usually a calendar year).

In modern economies, there are three main sectors of economic activity:

Primary sector: Involves the extraction and production of raw materials, such as corn, coal, wood and iron. (A coal miner and a fisherman would be workers in the primary sector.)

Secondary sector: Involves the transformation of raw or intermediate materials into goods e.g. manufacturing steel into cars, or textiles into clothing. (A builder and a dressmaker would be workers in the secondary sector.)

Tertiary sector: Involves the provision of services to consumers and businesses, such as baby-sitting, cinema and banking. (A shopkeeper and an accountant would be workers in the tertiary sector).

- Equity

a) It is the difference between the market value of a property and the claims held against it

b) It is also the ownership interest of shareholders in a corporation

Note: An *equity release allows elderly people to borrow cash against the value of their home,* without having to move. In a way, they mortgage their house to pay for a new loan…

See Private equity in the appendix

- Equity Returns

One of the most important profitability metrics is R*eturn On Equity* (ROE).

It reveals how much profit a company earned *in comparison to the total amount of shareholder equity found on the balance sheet.*
Note
A *shareholder equity* is equal to total assets minus total liabilities; it is what the shareholders "own").

Companies that boast a high return on equity with little or no debt are able to grow without large capital expenditures, allowing the owners of the business to withdraw cash and reinvest it elsewhere.
A business that has a high return on equity is more likely to be one that is capable of generating cash internally.

For the most part, the higher a company's return on equity compared to its industry, the better.
This should be obvious:
If you owned a business that had a net worth (shareholder's equity) of £100 million and it made £5 million in profit, it would be earning 5% on your equity (£5 / £100 = .05, or 5%).
The higher you can get the "return" on your equity (in this case 5%) the better.

- Escrow account
It is a third party account set up to hold funds usually in a bankruptcy, as a security measure to ensure relevant parties are paid.

- Exchange-Traded Products
They include:

a) Exchange-Traded *Funds* (ETFs)
Exchange Traded *Funds* are pooled funds that are bought and sold on the stock exchange in exactly the same way as stocks and shares.

Typically, each fund is set up to track the performance of *an entire index* by buying all the underlying stocks in proportion to their weighting.
ETFs subsequently allow you to track the performance of these indices through the purchase (and instant dealing) of *a single share in each.*
ETFs give an exposure to a whole index (lots of different companies).
Note: ETFs can have different structures, which will have implications on risk, return and liquidity. Examine the differences between them before investing:

b) Exchange-Traded N*otes* (ETNs) – which are *debt* instruments (not funds).
As ETNs are notes, ETN investors have direct counter-party exposure to the issuer of the note or to any third party that is guaranteeing the security's performance.

c) Exchange Traded *Commodities (ETCs)*
The recent development of Exchange Traded Commodities (ETCs) offers a new way of gaining exposure to the world of the commodities markets.

- Executive and non-executive directors
The *chairman* is the highest office of an organised group such as a board committee.

A C*hief Executive Officer* (CEO) or chief executive is one of the highest-ranking corporate officers (executives) or administrators in charge of total management.

A *non-executive director* is a member of the board of directors of a company who does *not* form part of the executive management team.

Note

The job of a non-executive director is to "oversee/watch" what is going on: *risk* taken and board *remuneration* for example.

- The 3 financial statements:

They are built to be used together to present a complete picture of a company's finances.

These three balance sheet segments give investors an idea as to what the company owns and owes, as well as the amount invested by the shareholders.

a) Balance Sheet

It is a financial statement that summarizes a company's assets, liabilities and shareholders' equity at a specific point in time.

It's called a *balance sheet* because the *two sides balance out*. This makes sense: a company has to pay for all the things it has (assets) by either borrowing money (liabilities) or getting it from shareholders (shareholders' equity).

The balance sheet is one of the most important pieces of financial information issued by a company.
It is a snapshot of what a company owns and owes at that point in time.

b) The income statement/Profit & Loss statement

On the other hand, the P&L shows how much revenue and profit a company has generated over a certain period.

c) The cash flow statement

It describes the inflow and outflow of cash throughout the period.

- Fund of Funds

It is an investment fund that uses an investment strategy of holding a portfolio of other investment funds rather than investing directly in shares, bonds or other securities.
This type of investing is often referred to as multi-managed investment.

- Futures price and spot price

Futures price is the price now for delivery in the future.
Spot price means on the spot/now … (*cash* price).
It is the price for delivery now.

- Gearing *(see leverage)*

The word gearing comes from its analogy with a gearbox (higher level) …

Gearing/Leverage is *borrowing money … It refers to debts.*
A company's gearing ratio is its proportion of assets funded from borrowing, relative to that funded by shareholders.

This term refers to the fact that spread betting and Contract For Difference for example, allow the client to buy (or sell) a financial product *with substantially less money than* the actual full market value of that financial product.

A company with a high gearing has a high level of debt in proportion to funds available from shareholders.

- Global macro

A strategy in which trading decisions are based on global economic and political factors, that is, macroeconomic principles.
The term global macro is used to classify the strategy of certain hedge funds; those that take positions in financial derivatives and other securities, on the basis of movements in global financial markets. The strategies are typically based on

forecasts and analysis about interest rates trends, movements in the general flow of funds, political changes, government policies, inter-government relations and other broad systemic factors.

- Globalisation

It is a worldwide trade and investment environment and the integration of national capital markets.

Globalisation and free market are the "enemies" of protectionism.

- Gold fix

It is the twice-daily act of setting gold prices by the five members of the London gold pool. This rate is used as a benchmark for pricing the majority of global gold products and derivatives.

Twice a day, the London gold pool sets the price of gold based on the basic economic principles of supply and demand. The world then uses these prices to determine the price of bullion and gold-related products.

- **Greenback** is a dollar note.

- Hedge/hedging

In finance, a *hedge* is an investment that is taken out *specifically* to *reduce or cancel out* the risk in another investment.

Hedging is a strategy designed *to minimize exposure* to an unwanted business risk (*to manage risk*).

The best way to understand hedging is to think of it as an insurance.

One common means of hedging against risk is the purchase of insurance to protect against financial loss due to accidental property damage or loss, personal injury, or loss of life.

Notes

- A reduction in risk will always mean a reduction in potential profits. Remember, the goal of hedging *is not* to make money but to protect from losses.

- *The cost of the hedge:*

Of course, nothing in this world is free, so you still have to pay for this type of insurance in one form or another.

Whether it is the cost of an option or lost profits from being on the wrong side of a futures contract – it cannot be avoided.

- *Some hedging techniques*

For an investor:

a) *Using Spread betting or CFDs* (Two derivatives)

It allows a *shareholder* to leave their *shareholding undisturbed* in the event of an unexpected price fall.

Ex: John owns a portfolio of mainly FTSE 100 shares with a total value of £40,740.

He thinks the FTSE 100 index is going to fall...

He could *physically sell* his shares, wait for the market to fall and then *buy them back* at a lower price...

However, he's got large gains on his portfolio and if he sells the shares, a *capital gain tax charge will arise*, together with *commission paid to the broker* ...

Instead, John decides *to hedge/to protect* his portfolio against a fall (*using spread betting or CFD) by selling* the FTSE 100 *index short.*

The idea is that if the FTSE does fall as expected, *any drop in the value* of the individual shares in John's portfolio will be *offset by profits* he makes by going short on the index.

So he *sells* £10 per point of the FTSE 100 future at *4074* points, when the quote on the index is 4074 – 4080.
As expected, the FTSE 100 drops to *3666*
If John closes his spread bet *by buying* the FTSE 100 at 3,666 his *gain* would be (4074 – 3666) x £10 = £4080

His portfolio losses would be matched by profits from his short position.

b) *Pairs trading*

A pairs trade or a hedge trade is one in which you go long on one share and short on another, *in the same sector.*
Action: You place an *up bet* on ABC and a *down bet* on XYZ

c) *Options and Futures* (Two derivatives)

The two most common *hedging techniques* used are *options and futures.*

In order to *hedge against indices*, buying or selling on a financial *futures market* such as Euronext.liffe, would be one method used…

But it's important to bear in mind that a broker offering *CFDs on indices* will normally *cover himself by buying or selling FTSE futures.*
He will add a spread onto the bid and offer prices that he is charged and will pass them onto you. That means that you would often be better off dealing in futures directly.

Usually *brokers* and *market-makers* hedge to cover themselves against possible losses; however some don't and try to "balance" their own book/portfolio …

- **"High Frequency"** trading (HFT)
It is done on high-tech computer programmes, allowing *breakneck speed trading*. See *"Quote stuffing"*
BlokCross is a pan-European high-frequency platform.

- **High risks examples:**
- *Too much leverage* from companies (investing with *borrowed money)* as a way to amplify potential gains (at the risk of greater losses)
- 100% lending (sub-prime mortgage for people unable to pay back) ...

- **Illiquid**
An illiquid market normally does not have enough volume (number of shares that changes hands between a buyer and a seller) for trading; so a small amount of business results in disproportionate price movements.
It has normally wide bid-offer spreads (difference between bid and offer).

- **Impairment**
It is a reduction in a firm's capital as a result of distribution (shares) or losses (defaults/written-downs).

- **Initial Public Offering (IPO)** - Flotation/public offering
It is the *first* sale of stock by a private company to the public. IPOs are often issued by smaller, younger companies seeking the capital to expand, but can also be done by large privately owned companies looking to become publicly traded.

In an IPO, the issuer obtains the assistance of an underwriting firm, which helps it determine what type of security to issue (common or preferred), the best offering price and the time to bring it to market.

- Inflation and deflation

Just like every other commodity there is a *supply of and a demand for "Money".*

Inflation is a *persistent increase in the level of consumer prices* or a *persistent decline in the purchasing power of money* caused by an increase in available currency and credit beyond the proportion of available goods and services.

Deflation is a *decline in general price levels*, often caused by a reduction in the supply of money or credit.

Deflation can also be brought about by direct contractions in spending, either in the form of a reduction in government spending, personal spending or investment spending.

Example:

Let's assume that we are on an island and there are 10 goods to sell and 10 £1.00 notes available to purchase them with.

We can safely assume that each item will end up costing £1.00 each.

If the quantity of money increases to £20 the price of the goods will increase to £2.00 - that is *inflation.*

If, however, the quantity of money decreases to £5.00 the price will fall to 50p – that is *deflation.*

What if instead of having ten items we build ten more?

We now have twenty items and only £10.00 so once again each item is worth 50p.

This form of deflation is the good type.

In fact if prices go down because the goods can be manufactured more cheaply this ends up increasing everyone's wealth.

Note: RPI (Retail Price Index) is used to set wages, state pension payments and benefits and deflation can lead to income cuts.

- Inside trading/dealing
Ask any trading/dealing participant where they stand on insider trading and you are likely to be met with an awkward silence…
As a criminal offence, no-one in their right mind is going to publicly admit to trading on inside information…
However, scrutiny of market activity just before major announcements such as takeover deals for example, reveals that some form of insider trading is almost certainly taking place…

But where should one draw the line between market normal gossip and inside information?
As a role of thumb, if information is specific and precise, price sensitive and *not in the public domain*, then it is fair to say that *this constitutes inside information...*

- Leverage or gearing
Leverage comes from "lever" as it gives you more buying power or *gearing* because of its analogy with a gearbox (higher level) …

Leverage is borrowing money …

It is also the *amount of debt* used to finance a firm's assets.
A firm with significantly more debt than equity is considered to be highly leveraged.
A firm's *debt to equity ratio* is therefore an indication of its leverage

Most companies use debt (borrowing) to finance operations.

By doing so, a company increases its *leverage* because it can invest in business operations without increasing its equity.

For example, if a company formed with an investment of £5 million from investors, the equity in the company is £5 million (this is the money the company uses to operate).
If the company uses *debt financing by borrowing* £20 million, the company now has £25 million to invest in business operations and more opportunity to increase value for shareholders, this is *leveraging …*
Leverage helps both the investor and the firm to invest or operate.

However, it comes with greater risk as leverage magnifies both gains and losses.

In spread betting and CFD, traders are highly leveraged because they put up a margin on the trade and their broker effectively lends them the rest.

The power of leverage
Example:
We've got £20,000 worth of securities bought using £10,000 of *margin* and £10,000 of cash.
Cory's Tequila Co. is trading at £100 and you feel that it will rise dramatically.
Normally, you'd only be able to buy 100 shares (100 x £100 = £10,000). Since you're investing on margin, you have the ability to buy 200 shares (200 x £100 = £20,000).

Cory's Tequila Co. then locks in Jennifer Lopez as a spokeswoman and the price of shares skyrockets 25%...

Your investment is now worth £25,000 (200 shares x £125) and you decide to cash out.
After paying back your broker the £10,000 you originally borrowed, you get £15,000; *£5,000 of which is profit…*
That's a 50% return even though the stock only went up 25%...

Keep in mind that to simplify this transaction, I did not take into account commissions and interest; otherwise, these costs would be deducted from your profit.

Now, say that instead of rocketing up 25%, our shares fell 25%.
Your investment would be worth £15,000 (200 shares x £75).
You sell the stock, pay back your broker the £10,000 and end up with £5,000.
That's a 50% loss, plus commissions and interest …

Think a 50% loss is bad? It can get much worse…

Buying on *margin* is the only stock-based investment where you stand *to lose more money than* you invested.
A dive of 50% or more will cause you to lose more than 100%, with interest and commissions on top of that.

What is a leveraged buyout or a "*bootstrap transaction*"?
It is using debt to get control of a company's equity.
It occurs when a financial sponsor (a private equity firm) acquires a controlling interest in a company's equity and where a significant percentage of the purchase price is financed through leverage (borrowing).
The assets of the acquired company are used as collateral for the borrowed capital.

Margin buying is a common way of utilising the concept of leverage.
It is sometimes called *leveraged trading* or *gearing up* because it requires less capital for the same exposure.
You only pay a fraction of the actual cost (margin) of the trade up-front.
For example, by purchasing a £100,000 worth of equities with only 10% down as a deposit, you are using just £10,000 to control a £100,000 investment.

- LIBOR

London Inter-Bank Offered Rate is the rate at which international banks lend to each other.

Libor is calculated every business day in *10 currencies* (dollar LIBOR, Sterling LIBOR, etc…) and 15 time spans, ranging from overnight to one-year based on the level at which banks have been lending to each other.

It is set and announced at around 11am in the UK.

It normally *sits marginally higher than the central bank rate.* It helps dictate the level at which lenders set rates on new mortgage deals.

For the Euro, the reference rates are the *EURIBOR* rates.

- **Liquidity** means cash or an asset that can be easily sold and turned quickly into cash.

- Liquid capital

It means enough assets that can *easily* be sold and *turned into cash* to meet payment obligations if the financial system was to freeze up …

- Liquid market

A liquid market has enough *volume* (number of shares that change hands between a buyer and a seller) for trading to occur without moving prices unduly.

See illiquid market

- Loco

It is the place at which gold is physically held and to which a particular price applies. Loco London – Loco London price.

- **Long** or "to go long"

It means to buy; as opposed to "go short" (to sell)

- Market Maker

A market maker can be an individual or representatives of a firm whose function is *to aid in the making of a market:*

He makes *bids* and *offers* for his account *in the absence of public "buy or sell" orders; in order to ensure market transactions are as smooth and continuous as possible.*

When a trader places an order to buy a stock which nobody is queuing to sell, market makers sell that stock to that trader from their own portfolio or reserve of that particular stock.

When a trader places an order to sell a stock which nobody is queuing to buy, market makers buy that stock from that trader and add it to their own portfolio and reserve.

In doing so, market orders are continuously moving, eradicating sudden surges and ditches due to buying and selling imbalance.

Market makers compete with one another to buy or sell stocks & options to investors by displaying quotes and are obligated to buy and sell at their displayed bids and offers.

An investor may be dealing with several market makers at once if that investor is placing a very large order which cannot be filled by the inventory of one market maker.

In reality, Market Makers make up the actual "market".

When a stock or option trader places an order with a broker, that broker fills that order by buying or selling with the Market Makers.

A Market Maker supplies a bid and ask price and then let the public decide whether to buy or sell at those prices.

Let's see what happens when we *remove* market makers from the markets:

XYZ stock is an extremely bullish stock who has just announced fantastic earnings…
You *want to buy* XYZ stocks but investors who are already holding XYZ stocks are *not selling*.
In order to attract a seller, you begin to bid higher and higher for XYZ stock until at last, a seller is moved to selling the stock…
This price could already be *extremely high*.

Now consider again a sudden bad news released from XYZ Company, creating a rush to sell XYZ stocks…
You *are queuing to sell* but *nobody is buying*.
In order to attract a buyer, you start to push the price lower and lower until at last, *the price bottoms out worthless…*

As we have seen, in an imbalanced buying and selling situation, market makers play an extremely important role of creating liquidity for prices in between in order to eradicate huge gap ups and downs and to ensure a liquid market for all.

How Does Market Makers Make a Profit?

Market Makers are not paid commissions to buy and sell stock options.
Most institutional market makers simply earn a salary from the marker maker firm that they represent.

On the trading floor, a Market Maker makes money by maintaining *a difference* between the price he would buy and the price he would sell a particular stock or stock option

This difference in price is known as the *Bid-Ask Spread.*

A bid-ask spread ensures that if an order to buy and an order to sell arrive simultaneously, the Market Maker makes the difference in Bid-Ask spread as profit.

Example
XYZ May 30 Call option has a bid price of £1.10 and an ask price of £1.30.
Market Maker John receives simultaneously an order to buy and an order to sell.
Market Maker John buys that May 30 Call option from the seller for £1.10 and then sells that same May 30 Call option to the buyer for £1.30, thus making £0.20 in profit completely risk-free

However, when a Market Maker is not confident that a stock can be so quickly bought and sold, due to the fact that there are only very few stock traders trading that security, then there is a risk that a stock which that Market Maker buys can only be sold when the market price is lower than the prevailing price, therefore resulting in a loss…
In order to protect against such a risk, Market Makers *widen the bid-ask spread* so that the transaction remains "risk free" to him over a larger price range.

Mark-to-market
Mark-to-market is an accounting methodology of assigning a value to a position held in a financial instrument *based on the current market price...*

Some people think banks are being overly punished by being forced to "mark to market" the investments they own; or price them according to current market value (instead of "fair value")
Example:
If an investor owns 10 shares of a stock purchased for £4 per share and that stock now trades at £6, the "mark-to-market" value of the shares is equal to (10 shares × £6), or £60, whereas the book value might (depending on the accounting principles used) only equal £40.
Similarly, if the stock falls to £3, the mark-to-market value is £30 and the investor has lost £10 of the original investment.

If the stock was purchased on margin, this might trigger a margin call and the investor would have to come up with an amount sufficient to meet the margin requirements for his account or close his position ....

- Merger and Acquisition

An acquisition, also known as a *takeover*, is the buying of one company (the 'target') by another.

An acquisition may *be friendly or hostile.*

A merger is a combination of two companies into one larger company. Such actions are commonly voluntary and involve stock swap or cash payment to the target.

A merger can resemble a takeover but result in a new company name (often combining the names of the original companies) and in new branding.

In some cases, terming the combination a "merger" rather than an acquisition is done purely for political or marketing reasons.

Note:

"Betting" on merger deals seems simple:

- Going long (buy) on the target company (the buyer usually pays investors a premium over the actual share price to gain control) or ...
- Going short (sell) on the buyer company due to anticipated cash outlay...

This is very well, but how do you know which stock to pick (except through illegal inside trading)?

A better tactic is to get to know a sector in which you think mergers are likely and invest *before* the crowd...

Note: When assesssing/analysing the *value* of a company (for a takeover for example), it is important *to take pension debts into account ...*

- Non-dom

Technically, one definition is:

People *live* and *reside* here but are not *domiciled* here …

A person who is resident but not domiciled is someone who is tax resident in the UK but retains important links with another country and has not decided to settle permanently or indefinitely in the UK.

It is said that a non-dom enjoys an unfair advantage but the non-doms are too "ingrained" in our cash-trapped economy to be thrown out.

No government can afford to turn its back on £10 billion in tax receipts …

- Novation – Confirmation - Affirmation

Note: Novation (English Law) or Assignment (New York Law)

In a novation, *with the consent of all parties*, one contract is entered into *substitution for* and *super session of another contract.*

Consent of all parties is a key ingredient for novation.

Remember the Clearing House definition:

A clearing house ensures that trades between a buyer and a seller are completed; *even if one party fails to pay …*

Novation refers to the process undertaken by the Clearing House whereby it substitutes itself between the buyer and the seller of a trade, acting as the "middleman" to guarantee the obligations of each party.

A *novation*, which is also known as *assignment*, is the process in which a counter-party wishes to *reassign* a transaction to a *new* counter-party.

The problem with novations is that the counter-parties involved are not always identified and communication is poor.
This lack of communication between counter-parties often means a bank makes a payment to the wrong counter-party, which creates payment breaks and leaves trades unconfirmed.

The *confirmation/affirmation* process refers to the transmission of messages among broker-dealers, institutional investors and custodian banks regarding the terms of a trade executed for the institutional investor.

Confirmation or confirmed
The *confirmation* that the bought or sold side of a Futures Contract or Options Contract has been:
a) Entered, acquired or disposed of *by* a Participant
Or
b) Accepted by Allocation *from* a Participant

Confirmation: a document identifying the details of a trade and any governing legal documentation, as agreed upon by both parties.
This document serves as the final record of the transaction.

Affirmation (of a trade confirmation): a procedure in a confirmation process, whereby a single record of the trade is created by one party evidencing the full terms of the trade and the counter-party verifies and agrees to that record.

Note: Affirmation of trade confirmations is *different* from trade verification (also known as economic affirmation), which is limited to principal economic terms.

- OECD
It stands for the Organisation for Economic Cooperation and Development

- Pari-passu
Two securities or obligations having equal rights to payment. For example, a secondary issue of shares that carry equal rights with existing shares are said to "rank pari passu."

- Pensions
We could say *private* and *public sector pensions (for civil servants, military personnel, firefighters, NHS personnel, etc)* have nothing to do with the world of finance …
However, pension funds invest in financial markets and are *dependent* on the good health and good results of these markets.
As to the *national state pension - £60 billion in 2010* - there is no fund invested and the government relies on income taxes.
It is a crippling cost to the state and the only option is that we all have to retire much later to fund it (and get it) …

- "Plain vanilla"
It is a term that refers to a relatively simple derivative financial instrument, usually a swap, an option, futures or bonds that are issued with standard features.

- PMI
The Purchasing Managers' Index is an indicator for economic activity.
A PMI over 50% is often taken to indicate that manufacturing is expanding; while anything below 42 % is bad news for the economy as a whole…

- Portfolio
It is a set of investments held by one investor; it is like a cake… For example, my portfolio may consist of: 22% in bonds (10% corporate and 12% gilts) – 28% in equities – 50% in commodities (10% in gold, 20% in cotton and 20% in oil).
A fund manager or a person may have/manage a portfolio …
It could be worth £1,000 or £1bn

- Pre-Pack Administration
The most *commonly used product* within insolvency services is pre-pack administration or Pre-Packing or Phoenixing.

Pre-Packing is the commonly used name for the corporate insolvency procedure known as Pre-Pack Liquidation.
Pre-Pack Liquidation is a process whereby the directors of an insolvent company start a new business which then buys the assets of the old failing business.
Instead of putting additional resources into an already insolvent company the directors are able to use the same funds to set up a new company and acquire the assets of the old.

The viable parts of the old business are transferred to the new company allowing it to begin to trade successfully without the weight of the old company's debts and other liabilities.
The *liabilities of the old business* such as outstanding debts and unfavourable lease agreements *remain in the old company* which is then normally put into administration and liquidated.

Because the new company seemingly appears from the remnants, or ashes of the old, this practice is known as *"phoenixing"*.
Phoenixing enables a company to start over again with profitable elements of the failed business, offering continuity for both suppliers and employees.
In a way, it is comparable to the breaking-up of the "good and bad "banks ...

Advantages of pre-pack administration:
- The Director's personal credit history is protected.
- Minimum disruption occurs and it is possible that some staff and customers may be unaware of the change.
- The sale of the business assets and undertaking is agreed in advance.

- The business may apply to trade under a variation of the original name.
- The existing company could eventually be dissolved by the IP (Insolvency Practitioner) as opposed to placing it in liquidation or bankruptcy.
This reduces cross-contamination of reputation and credit worthiness.
It then becomes a…Phoenix Company…

A phoenix company arises from the ashes of another.
The Directors of an insolvent company start a new company to buy its assets via an administrator or receiver.
This accomplishes the recovery of a business that has a viable core but is unable to repay outstanding debts.
It is a pragmatic arrangement that protects the interests of employees and private enterprise.

Benefits of a phoenix company:
- It reserves jobs for employees and Directors.
- It achieves a write-off of debt arrears (not subject to debentures or personal guarantees).
- It releases the business from contracts or leases that may no longer be required.

- Proprietary trading
Proprietary trading, proprietary trading desk or "prop desk" are terms used in *investment banking* to describe when the firm's traders actively trade stocks, bonds, options, commodities, derivatives or other financial instruments *with its own money* as opposed to its customers' money, so as to make a profit for itself.

Conflicts of interest in proprietary trading
There are a number of ways in which proprietary trading can create conflicts of interest between a trader's interests and those of its customers.

- Some suspect that traders engage in "front running", buying shares in companies the traders' customers are buying so as to profit from the price increase resulting from the customers' purchases and thereby harming the customers' interests.
- Some suspect that investment bank salesmen assist their firm's proprietary traders by encouraging customers to buy securities performing poorly after the proprietary traders have bought them for the firm.
- Lastly, because investment banks are key figures in mergers and acquisitions, a possibility exists that the traders could use *prohibited inside information* to engage in *merger arbitrage.*

So to prevent these possibilities, investment banks are required to have a *Chinese wall* separating their trading and investment banking divisions.

Note: 2010 – Volker rule: *Ban on Proprietary Trading* for US banks -
The rule also requires institutions to hold no more than 3% of their core capital in *hedge funds or private equity.*

European Union may follow suit …

- Quote stuffing

It is a practice where large numbers of stock orders are placed and cancelled almost immediately. See "*high frequency*"

- Re-capitalisation

Generally speaking, it is *a retructuring* of a company's mixture of equity and debt.
For example, a company may want to issue bonds to replace its preferred stock in order to save on taxes.
Re-capitalisation can be an alternative exit strategy for venture capitalists and leveraged buyout sponsors.

For example, a firm may borrow long-term funds (that is, it may sell bonds) in order to acquire the money needed to repurchase a block of its outstanding stock.
Because *re-capitalisation* will often affect the level and the volatility of earnings per share, *it is of interest to stockholders.*
Recapitalisation often occurs when a firm attempts to reorganise while in bankruptcy proceedings or to avoid a takeover ...
Re-capitalisation could also mean looking for *new capital* (by issuing bonds and rights issues etc ...) or *selling assets to pay debts or to increase the capital/debt ratio.*

- Renmimbi (RMB)
Renmimbi is Mandarin for people's currency.
It is the currency of the people of China whose principal unit is the *Yuan* (Japanese's currency is the *Yen*).
For many years, the renmimbi has been pegged to the US dollar (fixed dollar parity).

- Repo
Repo means *re-purchase agreement to borrow money* (like "repo 104" or "repo 27").
The deal is correctly booked as a *loan* under accounting standards ...
Note: Very useful to downplay the size of balance sheets... (temporarily selling assets and then re-purchasing them) - *before reporting periods* - allowing to give the appearance of a healthier cash position ...

- Risk arbitrage or Merger arbitrage
It is an investment or trading strategy often associated with hedge funds.
Two principal types of merger are possible:
In a *cash merger*, an acquirer proposes to purchase the shares of the target for a certain price in cash.

Until the acquisition is completed, the stock of the target typically trades below the purchase price.
An arbitrageur buys the stock of the target and makes a gain if the acquirer ultimately buys the stock.
In a *stock for stock merger*, the acquirer proposes to buy the target by exchanging its own stock for the stock of the target.
An arbitrageur may then *short sell* the acquirer and buy the stock of the target.
This process is called "setting a spread."
After the merger is completed, the target's stock will be converted into stock of the acquirer based on the exchange ratio determined by the merger agreement.
The arbitrageur delivers the converted stock into his short position to complete the arbitrage.

Example of Risk arbitrage simplified:
If "Joe's" taco shop was publicly traded at £50.00 per share, and "Sam's" taco shop moved to take over Joe's taco shop at a proposed £65.00 per share, this means Joe's taco shop's shares are instantly worth £65.00 per share.
The game comes into play because those same shares are currently trading at only £50.00 per share, should the buyout occur.
If the early trades (restricted or non-retail trades) elevate the value up to £60.00 per share, there exists the £5.00 difference.
This is the entrance of risk arbitrage.
The risk may be easily illustrated that there is a chance that the acquisition may not be completed and in this case the price per share will reduce to the original £50.00 per share.

- Securitisation
Securitisation is the process of pooling various types of debt like mortgages, car loans, or credit card debt, which are then sold to investors (see *CDOs*).

For example, mortgage-lenders bundle home loans together and use them to back bonds, which are then bought by big pension funds and other City investors.

It allows lenders to take loans off their balance sheets to free up capital - particularly useful for those that do not have access to savers' cash as a cheap source of funds.
You will probably not even notice if your home loan has been securitised.
You still make your repayments to the original lender.

Debts backed by mortgages are known as *mortgage-backed securities,* while those backed by other types of loans are known as *asset-backed securities*.

- Security
It is a negotiable instrument representing financial value.
Debt securities (e.g. banknotes, bonds and debentures)
Equity securities (e.g. common stocks)
Derivative contracts (e.g. forwards, futures, options and swaps).

- Short
To go short means to sell; as opposed to long (to buy)

- Short selling or shorting
It refers to selling an asset you do *not* own with the aim of buying it back cheaper at a later date. It is placing a down bet or a trade in anticipation of a *falling* market (see further down).

Naked shorting is when an investor sells the shares *without borrowing them first*, agreeing to deliver them at a fixed time. The seller buys the shares once the price has fallen and before he has to deliver them to the buyer.

Example:
Let's say you expect a falling car market...

- *Short selling*
You do not own what you want to trade ...

So you first *borrow* it, then *sell* it, then *buy it back* (when the price has fallen) and then *give it back* to the lender...
You first *borrow* a car, *sell* it at £10,000, *buy it back* at £7,000 and *give the car back* to the lender, together with a commission of say £1,000 ... *net profit £2,000*

- *Naked short selling*
You do not own a "something".
You sell *it even without borrowing* it first, then *buy it* once the price has fallen and then *deliver* it to the buyer at an agreed time.
You first *sell a car you do not have* at £10,000, then *go and buy it* at £7,000 ... and then *deliver it* at an agreed time ...net profit £3,000

- Sop
It stands for Standard Operating Procedure …

- Spot price and futures price
Spot price means on the spot/now … *cash* price.
It is the price for delivery now.
Futures price is the price now for delivery in the future.

- Sovereign bond
It is a debt security issued by a national government within a given country and *denominated in a foreign currency.*
It can be sold to the countries and foreign investors.

Under the doctrine of *sovereign immunity*, the repayment of sovereign debt *cannot be forced* by the creditors.

The only protection available to the creditors is threat of the loss of credibility (the sovereign debt rating).

- Sovereign debt
When a government is in short of money, it will issue its bonds either in its *local currency (called gilts*) or in *the international currency (called sovereign bonds*).

- Spread
It is the difference between the *bid price* (selling price) and *offer price* (buying price).

- Spread betting
There are many ways of trading a market:
- Physically buying/selling (equities, bonds, currencies, commodities etc ...)
- Using *derivatives* like Options, Futures, Warrants/Covered warrants, ETFs, CDOs, CDS, CFDs and spread betting.

Spread betting is a form of trading in which *you bet on the price movement* of a share, index, currency, commodity, bond and sports ... with only a *margin payment* (small deposit – sometimes as low as 10%) and where you pay no stamp duty or capital gain ...and no commission fee.
Note that you do *not* physically hold/own anything ...
You *borrow* it from or through a broker/investment bank ...and then give it back.
See appendix

- Statutory profit
It is an insurance term.
It is the total earned premiums minus total expenses and losses paid of an insurance company.

- **Stakes and shares** (difference)
- Real.com buys 15 million of *shares* at 6.27 yuan each from Shian company, paying 94 million yuan (£6.4m) for a *stake* of nearly one percent in the company.

- **Sterilising**

It is a "new word" created by the European Central Bank to quash fears the buy-ups of gilts will lead to a surge in inflation...

"It's qualitative *easing*, as opposed to quantitative"...

The difference between the ECB's quantitative easing and that being undertaken by other central banks, is that the ECB's purchases of bonds will be *sterilised — thus not affect the money supply.*

In other words, these sovereign debt purchases do not involve printing money.

The extra liquidity will be "re-absorbed" to limit inflation.

The ECB say these bond purchases will be offset by removing equal amounts of cash from the banking system.

- **Structured Investment Vehicle**

SIV was a type of fund invented in 1988.

SIV's were popular until the market crash of 2008.

The strategy of these funds was to *borrow money* by issuing short-term securities (e.g.bonds) at *low interest* and then *lend that money* by buying long-term securities at higher interest, *making a profit for investors from the difference.*

- **Sukuk (a sakk)**

Islamic bonds designed to get around religious laws banning the payment of interest for money lending.

- Swap rate

The "margin" is the difference between the interest rate that homeowners are charged and the *swap rate* is the *cost to the bank of borrowing* the money.

For example, if the average two-year rate is 4.55 % and the *swap rate is 1.26 %,* it means the margin is 3.29 % (4.55 minus 1.26).

See Appendix - Swap

- Tax

Do not confuse tax avoidance (which is legal*)* and *tax evasion.*

Tax avoidance involves structuring transactions, fundraisings, loans, business and balance sheets to make use of provisions and loopholes in UK tax law as well as in overseas territories, to minimize the payment of tax to the UK treasury…

Companies and individuals spent a fortune on experts to try and legally pay *less* tax …

They will call it "*tax efficiency*" ….

- Tier 1 capital

It is the *core measure* of a *bank's financial strength* from a regulator's point of view.

It is composed of core capital, which consists primarily of equity capital and cash reserves (see Basel accords).

Tier 1 capital is seen as a metric of a *bank's ability to sustain future losses.*

Tier 1 capital ratio

It is the ratio of a bank's core equity capital to its total risk-weighted assets.

During this turbulent time (credit crunch 2007/2009), every bank and every company in the land (and in the world) tried their best to increase their capital ratio (by selling assets/shares) *so as to survive …*

- *The "Triple witching experience"*

On the third Friday in March, June, September and December, options and futures of stock indices all expire.

So the nearing of the deadline can be especially volatile as traders in the expiring contracts scramble to close their positions.

As they do, their actions may push the market sharply up or down (giving some the odd fright) ...

- Underlying

In derivatives, the *security* that must be delivered when a derivative contract, such as a put or call option, is exercised.

In equities, the *common stock* that must be delivered when a warrant is exercised or when a convertible bond or convertible preferred share is converted to common stock.

The price of the underlying is the main factor that determines prices of derivative securities, warrants and convertibles.

Thus, a change in an underlying results in a simultaneous change in the price of the derivative asset that is linked to it.

- Underwriting

(Risk-takers used to write their names under the amount of risk taken).

It is a process by which investment bankers *raise* investment capital from investors *on behalf* of corporations and governments that are issuing securities (both equity and debt).

The bankers *assess the risks involved and assume liability* (any shares left (not taken/bought), *they will have to buy them*.

- Unwind (be unwound)

1. *To close out a relatively complicated investment position.*

For example, an investor who practices arbitrage by taking one position in stocks and the opposite position in option contracts would have to unwind by the date on which the options would expire.

2. *To rectify a transaction in which a mistake has been made.* For example, because of a misunderstanding, a brokerage firm may have bought the wrong stock for a customer. The firm must then unwind the erroneous trade by selling the stock just purchased and buying the correct stock.

- US non-farm payrolls

It is an important monthly indicator.

It keeps the financial markets on both side of the Atlantic on their toes…

It shows who are employed, how many are employed/un-employed etc …

- Vested shares

The meaning is comparable to "vested interest" (advantageous right which is securely held by a person or a group).

Generally, stock/share (acquired from your employer as compensation) *is vested* when you have *a right to keep it*; even if you can't sell it right away.

- Volume

It is the daily number of shares of a security that change hands between a buyer and a seller. Also known as volume traded.

- Warrant and covered warrant

Covered warrants offer retail investors the chance to do what institutions do with *options* – speculate with high exposure on almost anything.

A covered warrant gives the holder the right (*but not the obligation*) to *buy or sell* a specific amount of an equity, an index or another investment on a particular date at the strike price.

Placing a "call" covered warrants (an option to buy) or a "put" (an option to sell), investors risk no more than the premium.

Strike price
It is the price that the warrant gives you the right to buy or sell at.
Example:
For a £2,000 premium, let's buy 10,000 *call* covered warrants linked to the FTSE index with a *strike price* of £5,660 and a six month maturity.

The *break-even price* is where the difference between the strike price and the underlying price exactly equals the premium.
(The investor will not win or lose anything).
So £5,860 (200 points) is the *break-even* price since a rise of 100 points is worth £1,000.
If the FTSE rises above 5860 the investor will make a profit.
If, by the end of the six months, it is somewhere between 5,660 and 5,860, he will lose some money (because of the premium).
However, if it falls to 5,660, he will lose his original £2,000 premium (unless he sells the product to someone more bullish).
Notes:
- As well as pure *speculation,* covered warrants can also be handy for *hedging* positions:
If you thought that the index will *rise* over the next 12 months, then you could *buy a put* warrant on the FTSE 100 as a hedge.

- One of the main advantages of covered warrants is that, like spread betting and contracts for difference (CFDs), they are geared (see gearing), which allows traders to make a greater percentage profit than the percentage move in the underlying asset price.

The main differences between normal warrants and covered warrants are:

1. *Normal warrants* only have a company's stock as their underlying financial products.

Covered warrants can have a wide variety of underlying financial products.

2. *Normal warrants* are only issued by the company that issued the underlying equity.
Covered warrants are only issued by financial institutions (they take the actual delivery).

3. *Normal warrants* allow the warrant holder only to buy the underlying equity.
Covered warrants allow the warrant holder to buy or sell the underlying asset.

Difference between an option and a covered warrant:
- A covered warrant is just a long term option and is generally issued by investment banks.
- Options usually expire within 1 year but a warrant can last for up to 5 years.

- Sovereign Wealth Fund
A SWF is a *state-owned* investment fund composed of financial assets such as stocks, bonds, property, precious metals or other financial instruments.
Sovereign wealth funds invest globally.

- Write-down
A write-down is a *reduction* in the value of an asset; whereas…

- Write-off
A write-off is completely *removed from* a balance sheet.

- Yield
The yield is the rate of return on an investment; usually expressed as an annual percentage rate.

APPENDIX

The hedge fund managers

The private equity firms

What is a SWAP?

Some commodities
- **Oil**
- **Natural gas**
- **Electricity**
- **Gold**

The financial crisis (2007-2009)
- **Credit**
- **Causes & Consequences**
- **Sub-prime market**
- **The credit crunch**
- **Bankers' bashing**

Quantitative easing

Sovereign debts

Author's reflections

Spread betting

The hedge fund managers

What do these hedge fund managers actually do?
The simple answer is that they *invest money* - in anything that they think will make profits. They focus on generating "absolute returns" (or returns greater than zero).

Hedge funds embrace a wide variety of skills and strategies:

Long/short equity
They aim to profit from research and stock, picking skills by buying the best ideas and reducing the resulting stock market exposure by *shorting* (selling stocks they do not own) those they believe will perform less well.
See short-selling

Relative value
Typically they use computer systems to calculate the "fair" value of one asset relative to another and then *shorting* the more expensive asset and buying the cheaper one.

Event-driven
They seek investment opportunities surrounding corporate events, for example, investing in bankrupt or merging companies.

One of their main tool is *"leverage"*(gearing).
Leverage takes the form of a loan or other borrowings (debt), the proceeds of which are reinvested with the intent to earn a greater rate of return than the cost of interest.

What is so special about hedge funds managers?
The return achieved by a given hedge fund manager will (in theory) largely be driven by that manager's ability (or skill), rather than by underlying economic or market conditions.

The main reasons for this are:
Hedge fund managers generally try to remove some market exposure and aim to produce a positive return irrespective of market direction.
Often this will involve making an offsetting bet to *hedge against losing money on the original investment position.*

One feature often attributed to hedge funds is the widespread *use of derivatives* - bets on the future direction of an underlying asset such as a share, currency or even a whole financial market.
Some hedge fund managers will use derivatives almost exclusively, such as *Contracts for Differences (see CfDs),* rather than buying the underlying asset directly.
In some cases a hedge fund may do this to build up a *larger* investment position than they could afford directly - known as *leverage.*

However, the truth though is that the use of derivatives is commonplace in conventional banks, investment banks, insurance companies and the treasury departments of big companies.

So, for a fund manager, *leverage, shorting, hedging and derivatives are the key words ...*

The private equity firms

Private equity investors buy, improve on and sell businesses in an effort to make money from the *cash flow* the business produces and from the *capital gains* on exit.

Private equity investors (also called buy-out firms) *invest in non-public companies* and typically hold their investments with the intention of realising a return within 3 to 7 years.

Generally, *investments are realized through an initial public offering, sale, merger, or recapitalization.*

The process typically involves *a private equity fund-management firm* which *buys stakes,* in businesses.

The firm will often look for a business with an established market position *with strong cash flow*, a plausible *growth strategy* and clear *exit potential.*

The new ownership structure can supply the company with risk capital to *accelerate its growth*, by acquisition or to *re-structure.*

What do private equity firms look for in a potential acquisition?

- Strong management team.
- Ability to *create value.*
- Ability to generate *cash.*
- Significant growth potential.
- A clearly defined *exit strategy.*

What is Private equity *debt?*

This is a way of *raising money to fund a deal.*
Private equity firms do not stump up the cash for a takeover themselves. They prefer to raise the money by issuing lots of "IOUs" *(bonds).*

How does it work?
Private equity firms will sell these bonds to banks and pension funds and use the proceeds to either fund a big take-over or invest in high-yielding (high returns) assets, like home mortgages.

The owners of these bonds are *protected* as they theoretically *own a slice of the assets* that the private equity buys…

But some "buy-out" companies *delay paying back bond issues,* because they have invested in *risky home loans* … and as more and more people *default* on their mortgages, these loans *collapse in value*, forcing the equity firms to *halt the re-payment of the bonds* ...

Note:
These "buy-out" companies will insist that instead of destroying jobs, private equity deals turn out to be quite *beneficial not only for investors but also for employees*...
They first dismiss some employees but then, after having turned the company into a protitable and healthy one, they re-employed people…

A swap

We saw in the first part of this book that this derivative was an agreement between two parties to exchange sequences of cash flows for a set period of time.

Let's study *swaps* in more detail ...

The Swaps Market
Unlike most options and futures contracts, *swaps are not exchange-traded instruments.*
Instead, swaps are customized contracts that are traded over-the-counter (OTC) market between private parties.

Because swaps occur on the OTC market, there is always the risk of a counter-party defaulting on the swap

The two most common and most basic types of swaps:
The plain vanilla interest rate and currency swaps.

Plain Vanilla Interest Rate Swap.
Swap rates are used by banks to buy money from each other.

The most common and simplest swap is a "plain vanilla" interest rate swap.
In this swap, Party A agrees to pay Party B a predetermined, fixed rate of interest on a notional principal on specific dates for a specified period of time.
Concurrently, Party B agrees to make payments based on a floating interest rate to Party A on that same notional principal, on the same specified dates and for the same specified time period.
In a plain vanilla swap, the two cash flows are paid in the same currency.

For example, on December 31, 2006, Company A and Company B enter into a five-year swap with the following terms:

Company A pays Company B an amount equal to 6% per annum on a notional principal of £20 million.
Company B pays Company A an amount equal to one-year LIBOR + 1% per annum on a notional principal of £20 million.
The market for interest rate swaps frequently (but not always) uses LIBOR as the base for the floating rate.

For simplicity, let's assume the two parties exchange payments annually on December 31, beginning in 2007 and concluding in 2011.

At the end of 2007, Company A will pay Company B £20,000,000 x 6% = £1,200,000.
On December 31, 2006, one-year LIBOR was 5.33%; therefore, Company B will pay Company A £20,000,000 x (5.33% + 1%) = £1,266,000.
In a plain vanilla interest rate swap, the floating rate is usually determined at the beginning of the settlement period.
Here, Company B pays £66,000 and Company A pays nothing.
At no point does the principal change hands, which is why it is referred to as a "notional" amount.
Figure 1 shows the cash flows between the parties, which occur annually (in this example).

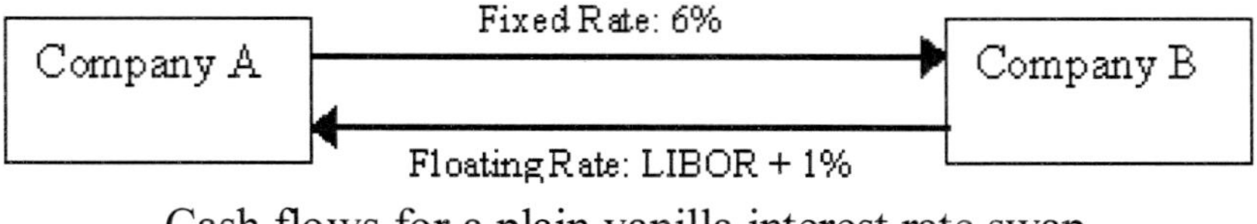

Cash flows for a plain vanilla interest rate swap

Plain Vanilla Foreign Currency Swap

The plain vanilla currency swap involves exchanging principal and fixed interest payments on a loan in one currency for principal and fixed interest payments on a similar loan in another currency.

Note: Unlike an interest rate swap, the parties to a currency swap *will exchange principal amounts* at the beginning and end of the swap.

For example, Company C, a U.S. firm and Company D, a European firm, enter into a five-year currency swap for $50 million.

Let's assume the exchange rate at the time is $1.25 per euro.

First, the firms will exchange principals.

So, Company C pays $50 million and Company D pays 40 million Euro.

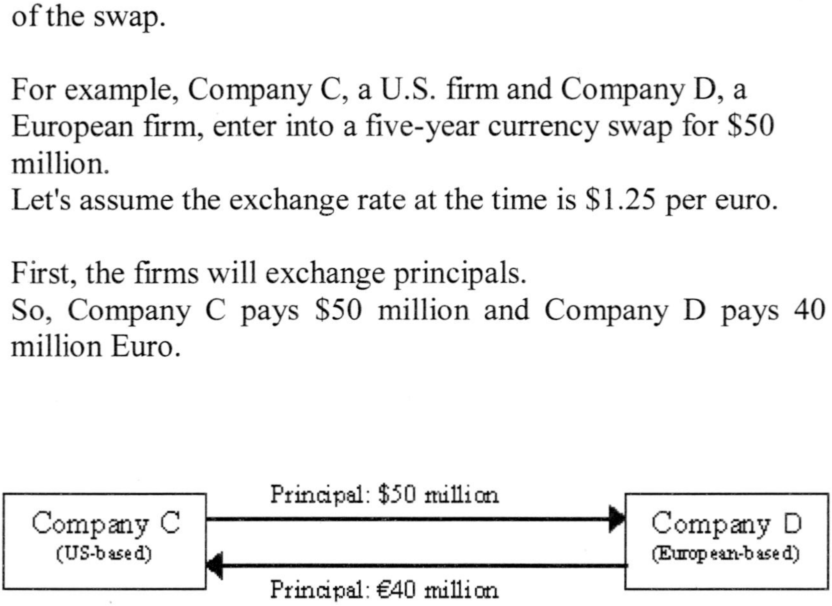

Cash flows for a plain vanilla currency swap.

Then, at intervals specified in the swap agreement, the parties will exchange interest payments on their respective principal amounts.

Conclusion

Swaps can be a very confusing topic at first, but this financial tool, if used properly, can provide many firms with a method of receiving a type of financing that would otherwise be unavailable.

Some commodities

Oil

Brent Crude (symbol LCO – Light Crude Oil) is the biggest of the many major classifications of oil consisting of Brent Crude, Brent Sweet Light Crude, Ekofisk and Forties.

Brent Crude is sourced from the North Sea.

The Brent Crude oil market is also known as Brent Blend, London Brent and Brent petroleum.

It is used to price two thirds of the world's internationally traded crude oil supplies.

The other well-known classifications (also called references or benchmarks) are the OPEC Reference Basket, Dubai Crude and West Texas Intermediate (WTI).

In its strictest sense, petroleum includes only crude oil, but in common usage *it includes both crude oil and natural gas*.

Both crude oil and natural gas are predominantly a mixture of hydrocarbons.
Under surface pressure and temperature conditions, the lighter hydrocarbons methane, ethane, propane and butane occur as gases, while the heavier ones from pentane and up are in the form of liquids or solids.

Note:
An *oil well* produces predominantly crude oil, with some natural gas dissolved in it.
A *gas well* produces predominately natural gas.

Natural gas

It is a gas consisting primarily of *methane*.
It is found associated with other fossil fuels, in coal beds and is created by organisms in marshes, bogs and landfills.

It is an important fuel source, a major feedstock for fertilizers and is environmentally friendly.
The by-products include ethane, propane, butane, pentane, carbon dioxide etc.

Liquefied natural gas
The world has enormous quantities of natural gas, but much of it is in areas far from where the gas is needed.
To move this fuel great distances across oceans, natural gas must first be converted into liquefied natural gas (LNG), called *liquefaction*.

LNG is natural gas that has been cooled to –162° C; changing it from a gas into a liquid 1/600th its original volume.

This dramatic reduction in size allows it to be shipped safely and efficiently.
After arriving at its destination, LNG is warmed to return it to its gaseous state and delivered to natural gas customers through local pipelines.

Note: An LNG spill *would not damage* the ground or leave any residues as it evaporates.
In water, LNG is insoluble and would simply evaporate.
LNG is not a flammable liquid, so it will not explode or burn.
However, like other fuels, when it vaporizes and mixes with oxygen, it is flammable if it is exposed to an ignition source.

Electricity

Electricity is difficult to store and *has to be available on demand.*
Consequently, unlike other products, it is not possible, under normal operating conditions, to keep it in stock…
Furthermore, demand and supply vary continuously.

There is therefore a physical requirement for a controlling agency, *the transmission system operator,* to coordinate the dispatch of generating units across the transmission grid.
This TSO uses fixed infrastructure (like pipe line and electric cables).

A wholesale electricity market exists when competing generators offer their electricity output to retailers.
The retailers then re-price the electricity and take it to market.

"Day ahead delivery"
The day-ahead price is considered the *benchmark* in the market, reflecting the *short-term* balance of supply and demand.
Average price is £55 per megawatt hour (2011).

Note
The *commodities* within an electric market consist of *two types: Power and Energy.*

Power is the metered net electrical output of a generator at any given time and is measured in Megawatts (MW).

Energy is electricity that flows through a metered point for a given time and is measured in Megawatt Hours (MWh).

Gold

Buying gold

The *troy ounce (ozt)* – from the city of Troy in France –
It is a unit of *imperial measure*. One troy ounce is equivalent to 31.1034768 grams.
There are *12 troy ounces per troy pound*, rather than the *16 ounces per pound* found in the more common *avoirdupois* system.
A full-size 400 oz *fine gold* bullion bar is worth about £250,000 (2011) …

But the purity of such bars can be guaranteed only if they remain in the vaults of a few specialist bullions dealers (London- Zurich- New York).

There are many alternatives to physically buying gold:

- *Exchange Traded Funds* are the simplest way for most savers to get exposure to the investment of gold.
EXTs track the price of a share index or of a commodity such as oil or gold.
- *Gold mining shares* - They are a more risky investment.
- *Gold stocks* are not gold. Rather they are *shares* in gold mining companies.
- *Gold stock options* are a contract between two parties that expires at an agreed-upon time in the future
- *Gold futures options* - All the bullion banks trade in gold options

Good Delivery bars

The original *verification* process is called *assaying*.
Bars which pass the strict scrutiny rules of bullion assaying are classified as *Good Delivery Bars* by their local professional bullion dealing community.
They retain this status as long as they are kept in vaults within the recognised gold bullion dealing community.
These bars are accurately assayed (original verification process: serial number - purity and weight) and guaranteed always *99.5% pure gold or better.*

Allocated versus un-allocated gold.

There is an *important legal difference* between the terms under which banks look after their customers' valuables:

Unallocated gold
Here the investor does *not* own specific *physical* gold but only a value 'backed' by gold kept in storage by a bank or company that hold the gold in “trust".
It is formally a deposit, which becomes the *bank's property* and its liability to you as a *depositor*.

When a bank sells you gold it is almost always '*unallocated*'.
You become a creditor - i.e. the bank owes you gold which you do *not* own.

Notes:
It is the most widely traded form of gold in the world and is considerably cheaper than allocated gold.
Banks encourage retail gold buying customers to remain permanently *unallocated* by charging fabrication, transportation and custody charges to customers demanding *physical delivery*…

As a result the *unallocated* system is now so successful that daily 500,000 ounces are traded inter-bank in London on an exclusively *unallocated basis*.

Allocated gold

Allocated gold on the other hand is different because you become the *outright owner* of gold and you are no longer a creditor.

It becomes your property and it cannot be used as the bank's reserve, so with allocated gold you get proper protection from systemic failure.

Banks cannot trade your *allocated gold* (your property) and it does the bank no good …

It obliges the bank to hold it as your *outright property*, under a custodial or safe-keeping contract.

If a bank goes bust, the liquidator will return your *property* (allocated gold) but not your *asset* (unallocated gold)…

Gold price

The *London Gold Fix* involves gold dealers from London's five biggest bullion banks establishing a common transaction price for a large pool of purchase and sale orders.

They do this twice each business day - first at 10:30am (the Morning Fix) and then again at 3pm (the Afternoon Fix).

The Gold Fix establishes the price at which the gross amount of gold on *buy orders* matches the gross amount of gold on *sell orders* - across all the participating banks.

No-one knows what the Gold Fix will be before it is declared.

The gold price set at the London Gold Fix is also used by large gold owners, including refineries and gold mining companies, to value their inventories.

Most central banks, such as the Bank of England, rely on the PM Fix to put a price on their stock of gold bullion.
Many retail outlets, such as gold coin dealers and gold jewellery manufacturers, also use the London Gold Fix to adjust their prices once a day.

The London Gold Fix is also used by *gold derivative* markets to put a price on various margined positions such as *gold futures, gold swaps and gold options*.

Spot market

Spot market gold is 'unallocated' gold.
Unlike the gold fix, the spot market is a *professional* market open all day.
It is inaccessible to private individuals.
There isn't anything to deliver or to keep (It is traded on balance sheets/on account)...

Gold certificate

Gold certificates are usually *unallocated gold* (undelivered) with an option to *convert into allocated* at the investor's option and cost.

Notes
- As gold is *priced in dollars per troy ounce*, it can lose some value in sterling terms when the dollar is weak...
- Investment-grade gold bars (or coins) are *free of VAT*.
- *Visit bullionvault*

Credit, the panacea…

Credit makes the world go round but it is also a hydrogen bomb…

"The first thing to understand is that *debt greases the wheels* of the capitalist free market" (Karl Marx).

The origin of credit …in America (where else?)

World economies are built on *credit* …
For anything and everything, the whole world needs credit ...
For example:

- To expand a company seeks a *business loan (credit)*...
- To be able to pay their suppliers, their staff, some traders at the end of the month need *bridge-loans* (*credit*) …
- To be able to build houses, a builder needs money from the bank and future buyers *(credit)* …
- Greedy individuals who buy beyond their means need *credit* (loans, credit cards)…
- Private equities to buy out companies need big *loans* from banks (*credit*)
- To buy a house people need *credit* (mortgages)…

- Even banks and building societies sometimes need *credit* to be able to lend us money...
  If they cannot get enough from their *customers 'saving accounts,* from the issuance of *corporate bonds* or by getting a short *loan* from another bank, *we have a money supply crisis*...

The financial crisis - 2007/2009

It is a misconception to think that governments have been *responsible for the credit crisis* (2007/2009); *they have not, except for their "laissez-faire" attitude towards the banking systems*...and *their "head in the sand" approach to the exacerbating economic crisis*...

Unfortunately, the problem has been that governments and banks went into dreadful financial difficulty *all at the same time.*

For years, *governments* over-spent and borrowed beyond their means through *gilts and sovereign bonds*.
Now they owe billions of pounds (sovereign debts)… and need to borrow even more only to service their debts …

In the UK 2011, with its trade deficit, huge budget deficit, its sovereign debts, public sector pension black hole (over a trillion), Public Private Partnership initiatives, etc … *the debt-burden government is in dire situation...hence a Treasury crisis...*

Whereas the *credit crisis* was the *result* of the nearly bankrupt banking system *caused* by the *banks* irresponsible and reckless lendings and "cunning" deals… as well as by their *bankers* being too "nervous" to lend to us or to each other…

This banking crisis did not help an already entangled Treasury that decided to bail-out the banks…

So "Credit crisis" or not, a "*Treasury crisis" was imminent anyway ...*

The author's conclusion:
Treasury crisis + Banks Credit crisis = UK Financial crisis

Financial crisis synopsis

The main causes:

Governments "Laissez-faire" attitude.
Debt-burden governments.
Reckless lending.
Sub-prime mortgages.
Sub-prime mortgage bonds.
Easy credits - Cheap loans.
Greedy individuals.

Not to forget some *credit rating agencies* (rewarding triple A ratings to *sub-prime* mortgage bonds) and to some extent, some *accounting firms* which were supposed to look through the books of the banks (while auditing)…
Nobody saw anything suspicious and sounded the alarm …

Consequences... Domino effect …

A financial meltdown

Several millions of sub-prime mortgage defaults…
Sub-prime bond CDOs and CDSs meltdown…
The downfall of Lehman Brothers in the USA…
Crisis of confidence …
Everyone has become suspicious…
Banks and investors started to panic…
Run on Northern Rock in the UK…
Banks and companies bailed out or going bust…
£ Millions of write-offs and write-downs…
House prices plummeting and high unemployment...

A credit crisis

A Sovereign debts crisis gripping Europe

The sub-prime mortgage market

The *sub-prime mortgage market* (US housing bubble) was one of the main causes of the crisis which has been crippling the financial world...

It involved terms such as: *Leverage - Sub-prime mortgages - Collateralized debt obligations* (CDOs) - *Credit default Swaps (CDSs) and* Frozen credit market (credit crunch)…

A family wants a house. So they save for a deposit and then contact a *mortgage broker.*
The mortgage broker connects the family to a *mortgage lender* who gives them a mortgage.
The broker gets a nice commission and the family becomes homeowner.
It's great for the family because *house prices have been rising for ever ...*

Investment banks and credit agencies involvement
One day, the mortgage lender gets a call from an *investment banker* who wants to buy the mortgage (the debt). … The lender sells it to him for a very nice fee …

Note
Mortgages as such are not "tradeable".
No trader or investor wants to poke around suburbs to find out whether the homeowner to whom he has just lent money is creditworthy.
Mortgages must first be turned into *mortgage bonds*; which are backed by a pool of mortgages with the same particular characteristics, of which, by the laws of probability, only a small fraction should default…

So first the banker turns these debts *into mortgage bonds*.
He then puts them in a little box and divides it into three compartments (Safe, ok and risky) and calls them *Collateralized Debt Obligations* (See CDO in the first part of this book).

Like any other CDO, a mortgage *CDO* works like a 3 cascading tray: Safe, ok and risky.
As money comes in (from the homeowners who pay their mortgage), the top tray fills first and then spills over in the middle and what is left goes into the third tray.

Then, as the investment bank has done all its good work, the *credit rating agency* "stamps" the top tray as a safe AAA rated investment.
The middle tray will get BBB and the bottom tray no rating at all as too risky (it is sold to risk takers like hedge funds)…
To make this CDO even safer, the banker will *insure* it (against default) via a CDS (*Credit Default Swap)*…

He then sells these mortgage bonds CDOs, to German or Spanish traders, to American or English investors like pension funds and trust companies, to Swiss banks, etc…
They buy into a pool of several thousands mortgage loans (on a pro-rata basis).

The *investment banker borrows* millions of pounds and buys thousands more mortgages, makes millions and pays back his borrowing...

This banker is so pleased that he wants more mortgages to create more CDOs.
But the broker can't find anyone …as everyone who qualifies for a mortgage has got one already …

So they come up with an idea…*which was a turning point ...*

Note
When homeowners default on their mortgage, the lender gets the house … and *houses are always increasing in value* (until now)…

So as they are covered if owners cannot pay their mortgage, lenders start *adding risk to new mortgages* by not requiring deposit or not asking for any proof of income…
So instead of lending to *responsible* homeowners, called *prime mortgages*, they started to lend to people *"less" responsible …* these are *sub-prime mortgages.*

Then, like the "prime" mortgages, these *sub-prime mortgages* are first bundled into *sub-prime mortgage bonds* and then turned into *sub-prime Collateralized Debt Obligations.*
The investment banker sell these triple-B-rated sub-prime mortgage bonds CDOs - *turned to triple A by rating agencies* - to investors like pension funds and insurance companies…

Not surprisingly, the home owner defaults on their sub-prime mortgage which at this moment is owned by the banker…

It means the banker forecloses (re-possesses) and one of his monthly payments turns into a house …
It is not a big deal as he puts it up for sale …

But more and more of his monthly payments (more and more defaults) turn into houses; *creating more supply than demand* causing house prices to plummet …

By this time the investment banker is holding a box of worthless houses.

Consequences:

- The *investment banker* panics because he borrowed millions to buy these CDOs, he cannot pay the money back and cannot get rid of them… (Investors have already bought thousands of these CDOs).

- The *lender* tries to sell off his mortgages but the banker will not buy them and the *broker* is out of work …

- To cap it all, for the *homeowner*, their investments are worthless …

- Everybody starts going bankrupt: banks, homeowners, companies etc… even the insurance companies that had sold billions of CDSs to investors (too many claims) …

So to summarize (from the turning point):

> Thousands of *sub-prime loans* → Bundled together to become *sub-prime bonds* → then repackaged into *Collateralized Debt Obligations* …which were given a triple A rating by some "corrupt" credit agencies so as → to be *sold to investors;* passing the risk that these loans would default on to them …

Then, worse to come! When there were no more loans to bundle, the big firms *created "synthetic"* CDOs *out of nothing, backed by nothing…*

That is why the losses in the financial system were so much greater than just the actual sub-prime mortgage loans …

… Whereas on the other side of the game, the same people were betting on the down-fall of these same CDOs … and were insuring them through Credit Default Swaps (CDSs)…

Credit crunch

So because of governments' "laissez-faire attitude", because of bad investments, greediness, negligence and recklessness banks and many companies have lost billions of pounds in write-offs and write-downs, have had to be bailed out, taken over or went burst.

During the financial crisis (2007/2010), banks had become so *burdened with debts (some still are)* - that they could not free up enough cash for new loans and mortgages – which is how *the credit crunch got its name.*

However, unfortunately, many companies that have avoided the worst excesses and have healthy balance sheets are now suffering.
They cannot get any credit to expand or help with their cash-flow…
House prices are plummeting and many homeowners are in negative equity and we are having a high unemployment ratio.
For people like you and me, it has become very difficult to get any loan (credit) to buy a property.

Maybe ...
The Islamic finance system, which introduces *greater discipline* into the economy and links credit expansion to the growth of the real economy, may be capable of minimizing the severity and frequency of financial crisis …

The Islamic system does not allow the creation of debt through direct lending and borrowing.
It rather requires the creation of debt through the sale or lease of real assets by means of its sales- and lease-based modes of financing.

“Bankers bashing”

Now, let me be the devil’s advocate

Bankers are not angels…

Ok, during the last decade, some bankers have been greedy and irresponsible in their approach to risk-taking …very often with their clients’ money…
Their motto was: “Heads we win, tails they lose!”

Ok, they lent *irresponsibly* and *prodigally* to anybody and everybody (without checking their credentials and credit worthiness)… Everyone was happy and nobody ever complained!

Collective responsibility
However, bankers cannot be blamed for everything and individuals, companies and the government must share some responsibility…

Furthermore now that they have to rebuild their balance sheets, sit on huge debts, increase their capital ratio (Basel III) and comply with tough new regulations, we *unfairly complain* that they do not lend enough…
Lend enough, really?... *Credit cards* (CCs) are *loans* and everyone has one, two or three cards…even if nobody forces anybody to spend, spend and spend on credit.
Everyone does know that CCs rates are very high …So it is for the individual to take their responsibilities and say “no, enough is enough”…

“Once bitten twice shy”
The reality is that banks do not want to take excessive risks anymore and will only lend to creditworthy companies and individuals.
They have become more “cautious” and more “responsible”…

Who could blame them for managing their risk more responsibly?

However, no government would dare to agree to the facts that:

- One out of three small businesses is struggling to stay afloat; with many needing a bridge-loan every month to pay their staff and suppliers; meaning that they are not financially very healthy and creditworthy.
- The same goes for many home owners who face severe difficulties in repaying their mortgage…
- Two out of three credit card holders are in the same situation…
- Many companies and individuals not only do they *borrow* but *need another loan to pay the interests on the first one…*

So, would you give these companies a loan???
Would you lend money to a "stranger" who was about to go bust or about to be made redundant or is in dire financial difficulty?

Let's be frank and honest; do we want the banks carrying on lending irresponsibly?

Furthermore *banks are companies* and as such, are primarily responsible to their shareholders … before their duty of care to their customers…
They have a business to run …

Like any other going-concerns, banks advertise in their shop windows for mortgages, business loans, bonds etc…
Ok, sometimes they lie about their products (like the advert on TV about anti-wrinkles cream…) but nobody forces anybody to buy their products.
We *have a choice* and no one *forces* us to get in and buy anything…

As to investment banks it is common knowledge they make big money for organizing right issues, initial public offerings, mergers & acquisitions and trading for themselves (proprietary trading – very often with clients' money)...
However again financially healthy companies have a choice and can shop around.

- *A word to the greedy individuals:*
Ok, banks do their best to persuade (to con?) us into borrowing and buying their products; but people are more than willing to take out a loan and spend it straight away; fully aware of the financial risk...

Excessive mortgages: 100% and 125% (often backed by fraudulent self-certifications) - 3/4/5 credit cards per person and thousand pounds owed – Big overdrafts (authorised and un-authorised) – Two holidays per year – Two/three TVs per household - Two, three cars per household - Every member of a family has a mobile (some have two, even three) - Secured and unsecured personal loans – Several computers per household - People buy big houses beyond their means and so on ...

For many people *credit cards* are a "*must-have*"... even if they can't afford them...

However, have you heard of the "furor" when somebody is refused a credit card or another bank facility? ...
Discrimination and unfairness become the buzz words.

Who is irresponsible here, the individual or the bank?

Quantitative Easing – The drastic measure ...

The theory
It is the modern way to "print" money; in fact, it is a virtual printing or electronic printing...

Quantitative Easing is a method of boosting the money supply. Its aim is to get money flowing around an economy (credit crisis) in a bid to lower bond yields, boost liquidity and lending.

The way to do this is for a central bank to buy assets in exchange for money.

The focus of quantitative easing is on *buying securities* (like government debts, mortgage-backed securities or even equities) *from banks*.

But where, you may ask, does the central bank get the money from to buy all these securities?
The answer is that it just waves a magic wand and creates it.
It does not even need to turn on the printing presses...

As every bank must hold some "reserves" at the Bank of England, the Central bank buys debts (or shares) from the banks and simply *increases electronically the size of their bank accounts by the same amount.*

The Monetary Policy Committee first embarked on a QE program in March 2009, after having slashed interest rates from 5% to 0.5% over the previous six months.
By the end of 2009 the central bank had purchased £198 billion in gilts, plus a further £1.5 billion in corporate bonds and £500 million in commercial paper.

As the banks' cash reserves expand, *they build up an excess of cash over securities.*
If they wish to redress this balance (and that's an important if) they have *to start lending out money* to other banks, individuals and businesses.
This will boost the money supply and inject liquidity into the economy.

Note: The Bank of England could have made this increased lending a condition of buying the assets; *but it did not...*

Worryingly, even if it (QE) doesn't do the job intended it could *dilute the value of sterling and kick-off inflation*, which would then *require higher interest rates to control it.*

The trick is for the Bank of England to say enough QE is enough.

Sovereign debts

Sovereign debts are government bonds *(gilts)* sold in its local currency *plus* bonds sold to a foreign country in international currency (*sovereign bonds*).
See bonds in the first part of this book.

Since 2010, a sovereign debt crisis is gripping Europe…

Greece, Ireland, Portugal, Belgium and now Spain are in financial trouble …and even Italy is not immune.

Over many years, these countries have over-spent and have accumulated massive debts...

Some governments not only have to *borrow money by auctioning their gilts* but have to borrow even more so as to *pay the interests on the borrowing*; more than 7% … it is unbearable and unsustainable…

European countries have a huge exposure to these sovereign debts and if a country defaults it may cost those a lot …

Now it is the day of *retribution* and *austerity packages are a must…*

Some of theses countries have needed an international bail-out from ECB and IMF… which have lent those billions and are buying their "worthless" bonds …

Credit rating agencies are watching and have down-grading some of them…which in turn means higher costs of borrowing and costly premiums to insure them against payment defaults (premiums for buying CDSs – credit default swaps)…

Author's reflections

Some European countries (like Greece) *may* find it easier and much cheaper *to leave the euro zone* and be allowed *to devalue* their *original currency* and use their central bank basic rates to control their flagging economies… which they cannot do while being part of the euro zone…

But even so, how to re-structure their *euro*-debts?
Defaulting may be the only answer available to them ...

Others (like Germany and France) may find it too expensive to keep bailing-out their debt-laden neighbours…

Just a few possible answers worth looking at:

A "two-tier" Euro currency…
A strong Euro currency consisting of fewer but strong economies…

Another possibility that may save the Euro is a universal European tax policy (a central treasury with direct/indirect tax policy).

The unlikely abolition of the Euro altogether…

To finish, let us play **"Spread betting"**

We know that it is a type of derivative (a financial instrument that is "derived" from an underlying market such as equities). It is a way of playing the stock market without actually owning any shares.

Advantages:

- One of the many advantages of spread betting is the ability to bet on prices going up (going long) and down (going short or short-selling) …and *leverage* (borrowing) …
- It is easier to understand than other financial instruments.
- The process is less complex than that for options, futures and Contracts for Difference (CFDs)…
- You can start with a small amount of capital
- You only pay a fraction of the full cost of the trade (usually 10% up-front). This is called *margin trading.*
- It enables you to profit from rising (bull) or falling (bear) markets.
- It is commission-free.
- Gains are not taxable and there is no stamp duty..
- There is no currency risk.
- It is anonymous

Cons:

- You incur your loss when you close the trade as all spread bets have an *expiry date.*
- Losses cannot be offset against capital gains
- Very important: You can lose more than your initial deposit or capital as the *margin trade* involved, means that while potential profits are magnified, potential losses are also magnified; *except for trades with stop losses.*
- With ordinary share, you cannot lose more than the amount you invested in the shares; w*ith spread betting there is no limit…*

How spread betting works ...

The basics

Spread betting is a leverage (borrowing) product. It requires much less capital (see margin) for the same market exposure.

Using shares as an example, the basic steps are:

- You ask for a "bid-offer" ("sell-buy") quote from a spread betting company.
- If you think that the shares are going to rise above the offer price, you buy (then sell later hopefully at a profit)
- If you think that the shares are going to fall below the bid price, you sell (then buy later hopefully at a profit)... see short-selling ...
- You tell them the size of the stake you want to bet, say £1 or £10, per point movement of the price.
- You tell them the total funds you wish to risk and place an appropriate stop-loss.

That's it!

What is short-selling (using spread betting or CFDs)?

It is selling securities you do not own (you must borrow them) in the hope of buying them back at a lower price in the future and pocketing the difference.

Example:

John thinks shares XYZ are going to fall from their current price of 450 p.

He enters a contract to sell them at 450p

As expected, the price falls from 450p to 400p ...

So he buys the shares back at 400p, making an 11% profit.

(450 – 400 = 50/450)

If his bet was for £10 per point, the profit would be 50 x £10 = £500

With shorting, the risk is that the price may move upwards during the period of the bet.

In the above example, if the price rose to 480p, John would have had to close his bet by buying at that price.

His loss would then have been 30 points (450 – 480) and assuming that the bet was for £10 per point, he would have lost £300.

Note

There are times when the order is relatively large and the broker hedges/protects himself by actually, physically buying/selling the equivalent (in the cash market)

NB: For any transaction, you need to go through a broker/investment bank …

* 9 7 8 1 8 4 4 2 6 9 9 0 7 *

ND - #0189 - 110926 - C0 - 210/148/13 - PB - 9781844269907 - Gloss Lamination